An Only Child

Also by Frank O'Connor

STORIES

A Set of Variations　*1969*
Domestic Relations　*1957*
Stories by Frank O'Connor　*1956*
More Stories　*1954*
The Stories of Frank O'Connor　*1952*
Traveller's Samples　*1951*
The Common Chord　*1948*
Crab Apple Jelly　*1944*
Bones of Contention　*1936*
Guests of the Nation　*1931*

NOVELS

Dutch Interior　*1940*
The Saint and Mary Kate　*1932*

CRITICISM

A Short History of Irish Literature: A Backward Look　*1967*
The Lonely Voice: A Study of the Short Story　*1962*
Shakespeare's Progress　*1960*
The Mirror in the Roadway: A Study of the Modern Novel　*1956*

AUTOBIOGRAPHY

An Only Child　*1961*

POETRY

Kings, Lords & Commons: An Anthology from the Irish　*1959*
Three Old Brothers & Other Poems　*1936*

BIOGRAPHY

Death in Dublin: A Life of Michael Collins　*1937*

An Only Child

FRANK O'CONNOR

G.K.HALL&CO.
Boston, Massachusetts
1985

The first three sections of this book originally appeared in somewhat different form in *The New Yorker;* and of the fourth section, Chapter 15 originally appeared in *Kenyon Review* and Chapter 19 originally appeared in *The Reporter.*

This paperback edition is published by arrangement with the Estate of Michael O'Donovan.
First published by Alfred A. Knopf, Inc., in 1961.

First G.K. Hall printing, 1985.

Library of Congress Cataloging in Publication Data

O'Connor, Frank, 1903-1966.
  An only child.

  Reprint. Originally published: 1st ed. New York : Knopf, 1961.
    1. O'Connor, Frank, 1903-1966—Biography.
  2. Authors, Irish—20th century—Biography. I. Title.
  PR6029.D58Z472 1985   823'.912 [B]   85-8515
  ISBN 0-8398-2879-9 (pbk.)

For William Maxwell

FOUR EPISODES from this autobiography have appeared in *The New Yorker,* and the author wishes to thank William Shawn and the other editors for their encouragement and assistance.

The frontispiece is a photograph of my mother, taken a few months before her death by my friend Dorothy Jeakins.

*   *   *

Throughout this book the author is referred to by his real name, Michael O'Donovan, not by the pen name that he later adopted.

Contents

MINNIE O'CONNOR O'DONOVAN

I

CHILD, I KNOW

YOU'RE GOING TO MISS ME

I

As a matter of historical fact I know that I was born in 1903 when we were living in Douglas Street, Cork, over a small sweet-and-tobacco shop kept by a middle-aged lady called Wall, but my memories have nothing to do with living in Douglas Street. My memories begin in Blarney Street, which we called Blarney Lane because it follows the track of an old lane from Cork to Blarney. It begins at the foot of Shandon Street, near the river-bank, in sordidness, and ascends the hill to something like squalor. No. 251, where we lived, is one of the cottages on the right near the top, though I realize now that it would be more properly described as a cabin, for it contained nothing but a tiny kitchen and a tiny bedroom with a loft above it. For this we paid two and sixpence—sixty cents—a week.

Up here we were just on the edge of the open country, and behind the house were high, windy fields that are now all built over. A hundred yards farther up the road the country proper began, and there a steep lane called Strawberry Hill descended past my first school into the classy quarter of Sunday's Well. The Women's Prison was at the foot of this lane, where it turned into Convent Avenue, and beside the Women's Prison was the Good Shepherd Convent. The convent had a penitentiary for "fallen" women and an orphanage, and it was in the orphanage that Mother had been brought up. At the foot of Convent Avenue on the left was a house where Mother had been a maid for eight years with a family called Barry, and where she had been happier than at any other time in her life. To the right was a shop the owner of which had once wanted to marry her. All these places were full of significance to me—the convent because my mother and I often visited it to see Mother Blessed Margaret and Mother of Perpetual Succour, who were her friends there, the Barrys' house because of the elegance of the life that Mother described in it, and the shop because of a slight feeling of resentment at the thought that if only Mother had been sensible and married a rich man I should have had a pretty elegant life myself.

That was the exalted end of Blarney Lane. At the other end it descended to the river and across the bridge to the North Main Street, where Mother took me shopping, and beyond the North Main Street, over another bridge to Douglas Street, where we had lived, and where my mother's brother, Tim O'Connor, had a cobbler's shop just across the street from Miss Wall. My memories of the cobbler's shop are hazy; I can remember my uncle only when he was dying in the South

4

Infirmary of dysentery he had contracted in the Boer War; and yet I seem to have a very vivid recollection of him—tall, thin, and fair-haired, unlike Mother, who was small and had very dark hair—because he seemed to be always gay. One of the things I have inherited from my mother's side of the family is a passion for gaiety. I do not have it myself—I seem to take more after my father's family, which was brooding, melancholy, and violent—but I love gay people and books and music.

Not that Tim had much to be gay about; his wife, as I remember her, was common and jealous, and disliked Mother's politeness and gentleness, while Mother never ceased to resent the hysterical scenes Annie O'Connor had made over Tim's grave. Mother disliked and distrusted any form of demonstrativeness, and when Annie married again 'it was only what Mother had expected of her. How she thought Annie could bring up two children unaided I do not know, but she and Father shared an attitude which seemed to be commoner then than it is now, of regarding all second marriages as a form of betrayal.

On the other hand, Tim had objected to Mother's marrying my father, Michael O'Donovan. The two men, who were old friends, had been in the British Army together, and were stationed at Charles Fort, near Kinsale, where Tim's girl, Annie, and Mother visited him together. Mother came back to visit Father. Though they were friends and drinking companions, Tim told Father that he was not good enough for Mother, and Father, to give him his due, did not hold it against him. "I'll get her in spite of you, Tim," he said, and he did. Certainly neither Tim nor my mother had much to boast of in their marriages. Maybe there is about these men and women of Mozartean temperament a certain unworldliness that makes them get the worst of any bargain.

Father played the big drum in the Blackpool Brass and Reed Band, and as I was the only child, I had often to accompany him, much against my will, on his Sunday trips to the band room or on band promenades at holiday resorts. The Cork bands were divided into supporters of William O'Brien and supporters of John Redmond, two rival Irish politicians with little to distinguish them except their personalities—flamboyant in O'Brien and frigid in Redmond. The Blackpool Band was an O'Brienite group, and our policy was "Conciliation and Consent," whatever that meant. The Redmond supporters we called Molly Maguires, and I have forgotten what their policy was—if they had one. Our national anthem was "God Save Ireland" and theirs "A Nation Once Again." I was often filled with pity for the poor degraded children of the Molly Maguires, who paraded the streets with tin cans, singing (to the tune of "John Brown's Body"): "We'll Hang William O'Brien on a Sour Apple Tree." Sometimes passion overcame me till I got a tin can of my own and paraded up and down, singing: "We'll Hang Johnny Redmond on a Sour Apple Tree."

The bandsmen shared our attitudes. There were frequent riots, and during election times Father came home with a drumstick up his sleeve—a useful weapon if he was attacked by Molly Maguires. There were even more serious incidents. Bandsmen raided a rival band room and smashed up the instruments, and one of Father's most gloomy songs listed some of the men who had done this:

> *Creedy, Reidy, Dessy, and Snell,*
> *Not judging their souls, they're already in Hell.*

6

Child, I Know You're Going to Miss Me

The night of the battle we'll show them some fun;
We'll hang up the ruffian that stole our big drum.

Almost all the bandsmen were ex-bandsmen of
the British Army, as Father was; and I think it may
have been something of a tragedy to them that when
once they returned to Cork, music became less important than the political faction for whom they made it.
Father was devoted to the policy and personality of
William O'Brien, who had married the daughter of one
of the great Franco-Jewish bankers. It was Sophie
Raffalovitch's mother who had started the romance
by sending to O'Brien when he was in gaol a verse
of Racine with an eagle's feather enclosed, but I am
glad that when Sophie O'Brien was old and poor in
France during the German occupation, the Irish Government protected her and paid her an allowance.
Once, when there were threats of a Molly Maguire
attack, Father, an enormously powerful man, acted as
bodyguard for William O', and William O' thanked him
personally and handed him a pound note. All the same,
for several years Father had been big drummer of a
Molly Maguire band. It was a superb band, and Father
liked music so well that he preferred it to politics. For
the sake of the music he even endured the indignity of
playing for Johnny Redmond. Naturally, whenever he
attended a demonstration at which William O' was
criticized, he withdrew, like a good Catholic from a
heretical service. What made him leave the Molly band
and join the Blackpool Band I never knew. It was a
period that for some reason he never liked to talk about,
and I suspect that someone in the band must have
impugned him by calling him a turncoat. That is the
sort of thing that would have broken his spirit, for he
was a proud man and a high-principled one, though

7

what his principles were based on was more than I ever discovered. He was the one who insisted on the "O'Donovan" form of the name, and it must have been his absence at the Boer War that explains my being described as "Donovan" on my birth certificate. He would not permit a slighting reference to William O'Brien, and reading the *Echo,* the only evening paper in Cork, and a Molly one, was as much a torment as a pleasure to him. "There were about 130 people present, most of them women, with a sprinkling of children" was how the *Echo* would describe any meeting of O'Brien's, and Father would raise his eyes to Heaven, calling on God to witness that anything the *Echo* said was untrue. "Oh, listen to George Crosbie, the dirty little caffler!" he would cry with mortification. In days when no one else that I knew seemed to worry about it, he was a passionate believer in buying Irish manufactures, and often sent me back to the shop with a box of English matches that had been passed off on me. He was a strong supporter of Jim Larkin, the Irish Labour leader; for months when he was out on strike we practically didn't eat, but we always bought *The Irish Worker*, Larkin's paper, and I was permitted to read it aloud because my dramatic style of reading suited Larkin's dramatic style of journalism. According to Mother, there was a period in my infancy when Father didn't drink for two years. He had drunk himself penniless, as he frequently did, and some old friend had refused him a loan. The slight had cut him so deep that he stopped drinking at once. The friend was wrong if he assumed that Father would not have repaid that or any other loan, but, still, it was a great pity that he hadn't a few more friends of the sort.

It was no joke to go with Father on one of his Sunday outings with the band, and I often kicked up hell about it, but Mother liked me to go, because she had some strange notion that I could restrain him from drinking too much. Not that I didn't love music, nor that I wasn't proud of Father as, with the drum slung high about his neck, he glanced left and right of it, waiting to give the three taps that brought the bandsmen in. He was a drummer of the classical type: he hated to see a man carry his drum on his belly instead of his chest, and he had nothing but scorn for the showy drummers who swung or crossed their sticks. He was almost disappointingly unpretentious.

But when he was on the drink, I was so uncertain that I always had the feeling that one day he would lose me and forget I had been with him at all. Usually, the band would end its piece in front of a pub at the corner of Coburg Street. The pubs were always shut on Sunday until after last Mass, and when they opened, it was only for an hour or two. The last notes of "Brian Boru's March" would hardly have been played before Father unslung the drum, thrust it on the young fellows whose job it was to carry it, and dashed across the road to the pub, accompanied by John P., his great buddy. John P.—I never knew what his surname was—was a long string of misery, with an air of unutterable gravity, emphasized by the way he sucked in his cheeks. He was one of the people vaguely known as "followers of the band"—a group of lonely souls who gave some significance to their simple lives by attaching themselves to the band. They discussed its policies and personalities, looked after the instruments, and knew every pub in Cork that would risk receiving its members after hours. John P., with a look of intense concentration, would give a secret knock on the side door of the pub and utter what seemed to be whispered endearments through the keyhole, and more and more bandsmen

9

would join the group peppering outside, while messengers rushed up to them shouting: "Come on, can't ye, come on! The bloomin' train will be gone!"

That would be the first of the boring and humiliating waits outside public houses that went on all day and were broken only when I made a scene and Father gave me a penny to keep me quiet. Afterwards it would be the seaside at Aghada—which wasn't so bad because my maternal grandmother's people, the Kellys, still lived there and they would give me a cup of tea—or Crosshaven, or the grounds of Blarney Castle, and in the intervals of playing, the band would sit in various public houses with the doors barred, and if I was inside I couldn't get out, and—what was worse for a shy small boy—if I was out I couldn't get in. It was all very boring and alarming, and I remember once at Blarney, in my discouragement, staking my last penny on a dice game called the Harp, Crown, and Feather in the hope of retrieving a wasted day. Being a patriotic child, with something of Father's high principle, I put my money on the national emblem and lost. This was prophetic, because since then I have lost a great many pennies on the national emblem, but at least it cured me of the more obvious forms of gambling for the rest of my days.

On another occasion, after what had seemed an endless day in Crosshaven, I found myself late at night outside a locked public house in Cork opposite the North Cathedral, waiting for some drunk to emerge, so that I could stick my head in the door and wail: "Daddy, won't you come home now?" At last, in despair, I decided to make my own way home through the dark streets, though I had never been out alone at night before this. In terror, I crept down the sinister length of Shandon Street, and crossed the street so that I might escape seeing what I might see by the old grave-

yard, and then, at the foot of Blarney Lane, I saw a
tiny shop still open. There were steps up to the hall
door, and railings round the area, and the window was
small and high and barely lighted by one oil lamp inside,
but I could plainly see a toy dog in it, looking out at me.
Praying that it wouldn't be beyond my means, I climbed
up the steps. Inside, a door on the right led from the
hall to the shop, where the counter was higher than
my head. A woman came out of the little back room
and asked me what I wanted. I told her I wanted to
know the price of the dog, and she said it was sixpence.
I had earned a lot of pennies by standing outside public
houses that day, and sixpence was exactly what I had,
so I threw it all on the counter and staggered out,
clutching my protector. The rest of the way up Blarney
Lane I walked without fear, setting my woolly dog at
every dark laneway to right and left of me with a fierce
"At 'em, boy!" Fortunately for myself, I was fast asleep
when Father arrived home, distracted over losing me.

As for keeping him off the drink, I never did it but
once, when I drank his pint, became very drunk,
smashed my head against a wall, and had to be steered
home by himself and John P., both of them mad with
frustration and panic, and be put to bed.

Father had been brought up in the vicinity of
Cork Barracks, a mile or two away at the other side of
the town, and his family still lived there. For this neighbourhood he seemed to pine as an Irish immigrant in
Brooklyn is supposed to pine for Galway Bay, though,
unlike the Brooklyn immigrant, Father meant it. He
used to take me to my grandparents' house in Harrington's Square—an uneven unlighted piece of ground
between the Old Youghal Road and the Ballyhooley
Road that seemed to have been abandoned by God and
was certainly abandoned by the Cork Corporation. One

side was higher than the other, and a channel had been hollowed out before the houses on the lower side to give ingress, while at the end of this one lonesome pillar commemorated some early dream of railing the place off. In England such sites are politely known as "non-adopted," a word that well suits their orphaned air. It was inhabited largely by washerwomen who worked mainly for the British officers in Cork Barracks, and there were three sets of iron poles in the middle of the square to support their lines. One set belonged to my grandmother, a stout, coarse peasant woman from Aghada, who flopped about the floor in bare feet because these were what she was used to and the boots still continued to give her trouble. She had a pronounced Mongolian appearance, and the protrusion of the brows and the high cheekbones gave her a constant look of peering at things. With it went a curious shrugging of the shoulders, which I never noticed again till I saw it in an eminent writer and traced it down to a common dislike of soap and water. After a huge meal of stockfish and boiled potatoes she would shrug and bless herself and then add her own peculiar grace: "Well, thanks be to God, we're neither full nor fasting." I remember little of my grandfather, a quiet, bearded old man. My aunt was a deaf-mute, and during the early part of my childhood I met her only once or twice, when she was home on holidays from Glasgow, where she lived with her husband—a tailor named Hanlon. She, too, seemed to pine for the old spot.

I had no nostalgia for it. The kitchen of my grandparents' house resembled that of a country cabin, and there was nothing in it but a table and a few chairs— no pictures, or anything else that could hold the attention of a child. It was criss-crossed with clotheslines, and in wet weather it smelled of damp linen and was warm with a big fire where the heaters for the box-iron were reddened. (I liked the heaters, and I wished Mother would get a box-iron instead of her own little flat-iron.)

Hospitality there was of the same order: strictly functional, and with none of the frills of cakes and jam that a child remembers. Sometimes my Uncle Laurence, my father's brother, came in, and Grandmother was sent out to the pub and returned with a great jug of porter under her old plaid shawl, and this was mulled with the big iron poker, and I was given half a mug of it with sugar. One night when I was about three or four and sitting on Father's knee, almost asleep, he suddenly put me down, lifted the poker, and slashed my uncle's face across with it. I remember the long red line on my uncle's face, which suddenly went white, and blood beginning to pour from it, and the quiet voice in which he said: "Mick Donovan, if another man in the world did that to me, I'd have his life." * Laurence was the only member of the family I liked, and the scene made a terrifying impression on me.

I can only have been five or six when a house fell vacant next door to my grandparents'. Mother did not want to take it; it would detach her from the convent, which was one of the nearest things she knew to a home, and from the neighbours in Blarney Lane, whom she liked and who liked her. It was probably characteristic of the orphan, but I never met anyone so firmly rooted in places and people. When she began visiting me in Dublin, she was at first very lonely; then she noticed a house that reminded her of one in Cork, and then she saw a woman with a child who reminded her

---

* When I was growing up, "O'Donovan" and "Donovan" were almost interchangeable. English officials insisted on the latter form, and it was always used familiarly.

of a neighbour in Cork, and she even observed a piece of furniture in a shop-window that reminded her of something we had once possessed, till at last she built up a world of remote analogies with comfortable and friendly memories that protected her from the unknown. She disliked my father's family even more than I did, and, besides, the rent—four and sixpence a week—was nearly twice what we paid for the little cottage in Blarney Lane. But Father was homesick for the delights of the Barrack Stream (as the old people called the locality), and he argued irritably that with a commodious house like that—four rooms instead of two—we could take in lodgers, and everyone knew the big money you could make out of lodgers. So one day we said good-bye sadly to the old neighbours, piled all our possessions on a little donkey cart, and set out after them down Blarney Lane toward the river. I carried the kitten in my arms.

That night Mother sat in the dirty, dilapidated kitchen of the new house and wept, but Father's family were happily reunited in a neighbourhood where they were well known and—according to themselves—highly respected. At least, in Barrack Stream, Father was sure of a good funeral. Grandfather and Grandmother lived next door, my Uncle Laurence and his family lived up the Old Youghal Road, near Mayfield Chapel, and for a time my deaf-and-dumb aunt and her deaf-and-dumb husband lodged with the old people in the house next door. The homesickness of my father's family was really quite remarkable.

Barrack Stream, though richer than Blarney Lane, was rougher, like all places attached to military barracks. There were women who went with soldiers, and girls who went with officers, and sinister houses where people drank after hours. Of course, it had its advantages for me, particularly when we weren't plagued by lodgers. (Of these I remember two lots—a family so brutal and filthy that at last Father, who was out for most of the day and only pooh-poohed Mother's complaints, practically ejected them himself, and an old lady so scared of drafts that she nailed up the window and padded the door till the front room stank.) A lot of the time I had an attic to myself, where I could keep my treasures, and there was an outdoor toilet, with a door suitable for climbing. From the roof of this I could get on to the high back wall and command a view of the neighbours' back yards and of the hillside opposite as it sloped down into the valley of the city. I sometimes sat there for hours, till darkness crept up on me, and in order to enjoy the view a little longer I even climbed out of the attic window and up the roof to the ridge-pole. Besides, there was the Barracks, and the day was punctuated by bugle calls, and sometimes the soldiers went by on a route march, preceded by their band. When this happened in the evening and Father was at home, we both dashed for the front door. The regiments at the Barracks were always changing, and while the fast girls compared lovers—English, Scotch, and Welsh—Father compared the height and smartness of the men, the quality of the band, and, of course, the big drummers. If you went far enough afield, you could even see an occasional military funeral, with a gun-carriage draped in the Union Jack, and a band that played Chopin's Funeral March. With the O'Donovan morbidity, I loved military funerals, and when Father was in good humour I got him to hum dead marches for me. Though he was usually ready to oblige with Chopin, Handel, or Beethoven, he maintained that the greatest of dead marches was "The Flowers of the Forest" as played by the pipe band of the

Scots Guards. Naturally, he performed all these as though the principal instrument were the big drum, and I tested them out, pacing the kitchen with reversed sweeping brush, lost in ecstatic melancholy. Afterwards he would be bound to sing me "The Burial of Sir John Moore," one of his favourite songs and mine. So far as music went, he and I got on excellently.

But the move to Barrackton brought to a head my sense of the conflict between the two families whose heredity I shared. The more I saw of my grandparents, the less I liked them. Children, who see only one side of any question and because of their powerlessness see this with hysterical clarity, are abominably cruel. And an only child is worse. There was no way in which I could have avoided seeing the contrast between my mother, on the one hand, and the women of my father's family on the other, and it meant nothing to me that one was old, another ill, another deaf-and-dumb.

Mother was dainty in everything she did. Women can observe and describe that sort of fastidiousness better than men, and my cousin's wife, whom Mother adored, gives a tart and amusing description of her at the age of eighty-five, flouncing about the kitchen of May's little house, demanding to be inspected and assured that her hat was not crooked or her skirt too short. When she returned from town, she would immediately take off her wet shoes, stretch them with her hands, stuff them with newspapers (she had never been able to afford shoe-trees), and set them to dry before the fire. Only then would she produce the perfect pear or the perfect peach that she had coveted in some fruit-shop window, not for herself but May. This is the side of her I remember best, because one of my earliest recollections of her is the way she would choose a twopenny Christmas card, study it, price it, put it

back, return and study it again with a frown as though
she were wondering if it really was a Rembrandt etch-
ing, though all the time she was thinking not of what
it was but of its appropriateness to the person she was
buying it for.

Besides, she was an excellent cook and a first-rate
housekeeper, a woman to whom cleanliness and neat-
ness came as natural as untidiness does to me. Though,
apart from our beds, the only furniture we had was
what went into the kitchen, she made even that room
look beautiful. Over the mantelpiece hung a long mirror, and to the right of it the lamp. At either side of the
window were pictures of the Battle of Bethlehem, a
Boer War relic which I searched by the hour for a likeness of Father, and of Kathleen Mavourneen, with
insets of the Lakes of Killarney. Facing the window
was the little sideboard with one of our two clocks, and
between that and the door was the bedroom wardrobe,
which was too big to go up the stairs. Father used the
top of it for his own treasures, his razors, clippers, and
pipes.

One of those peculiar romances of Mother's that
I was always so curious about—not being very satisfied
with the father she had supplied me with—had been
with a French chef called Armady who had taught her
to make superb coffee. I think he must also have taught
her to hate fried food, that curse of Irish life, because
the first thing she bought when I got a job and turned
my wages over to her was a gas-stove on which she
could grill. In the evenings, when I induced Father and
herself to sing for me, his favourites were sentimental
songs like "Eileen Alannah" and "Kathleen Mavourneen," and these he sang in the manner of a public-
house singer, all sniffle and rallentando. When Mother
was not singing Moore's melodies—her favourites were

"How Dear to Me the Hour When Daylight Dies," "Farewell But Whenever You Welcome the Hour," and "I Saw from the Beach"—she sang charming little drawing-room songs of the Victorian period like "The Danube River," "Alabama Moon," "When the Old Man Died," and "Three Students Went Merrily over the Rhine," and she sang them in good time, in a sweet, clear, girlish voice. It was, I suppose, typical of me that when I sang the same songs I tried to invest them with Father's trills, but I got ticked off for it. Even when I sang with her as a grown man I got a sharp "No!" when I strayed from the correct time. Her harshest criticism was an impatient "Ah, you have it out loud and all wrong."

She was the sort of woman who is always called in when there is trouble in a house, and as she had to bring me with her in the years when I was still an infant, some of my earliest recollections of her are so extraordinary that to this day I cannot say if they weren't hallucinations. Once, when we were living in Blarney Lane, she carried me to a neighbour's house and put me sitting on a chair by the door. I could see into the little partitioned-off bedroom, and I watched her, in the candlelight, holding up the head of a young man who was coughing red stuff on to the bed. In a loud voice Mother said something that sounded like prayers, and he continued to cough till all the bedclothes were bright red, and then he seemed to fall asleep, and she laid him back on the pillow and knelt beside him, praying into his ear. Another time she took me with her and I saw a young man crouching under the bedroom window with his hands raised, screaming: "They'll never get me alive!" Mother went up to him, smiling, her two hands out in the gesture that was most characteristic of her, murmuring reproachfully: "Ah,

Johnny, Johnny, don't you know who it is? It's only Mrs. Donovan." The strange quality of these half-memories of her is best summed up in one incident. I remember the mother of a very sick little girl coming hysterically to the door and our running back with her to the cottage, where Mother forced back the child's rectal passage, which had become extruded. The incident is perfectly clear in my mind, though I do not even know if what I think I saw is physically possible.

She had always wanted to be a nurse and was an excellent one. When Grandfather was dying, it was she who looked after him, and I watched her scrubbing the floor, killing the lice that covered the bedroom wall, and changing the bedclothes, while downstairs Grandmother, huge, shiftless, and dirty, drained her mug of porter over the fire and moaned. "I'm a bird alone, a bird alone!" she whined, and Mother, sick with disgust, told her sharply that she could at least wash her face before the priest came.

When my grandmother came to live with us after Grandfather's death, I nearly lost my mind. Lodgers were awful, and the large fortunes to be made from them were clearly illusory, but at least they were not relations and I did not have to apologize for them to any other kid I brought to the house and wanted to impress. I was always trying to make an impression, particularly on one friend, Bob O'Connell, whose father was a colour sergeant and who spoke in a cultured English voice that I tried hard to imitate, but when I glanced into the kitchen and saw Grandmother at one of her modest repasts—a mess of hake and potatoes boiled in a big pot, with the unpeeled potatoes afterwards tossed on the table to be dipped in a mound of salt and eaten out of the fingers, and a jug of porter beside these—I fled for very shame. And once, when

Mother was at work and Grandmother was supposed to give me my dinner, I hid under the kitchen table, yelling bloody murder and refusing to come out until Mother returned and fed me herself. Mother tried to induce her to keep herself clean, but Grandmother, deeply offended, shrugged herself in her dirty old clothes, blinked her eyes, and retorted sullenly: "Sure, what is it but clean dirt?"

I had already become the classic example of the Mother's Boy. Later when as a public official I had to be careful not to involve my employers in my literary activities and had to change my name, I took her name in place of my own. At that time all I could do was beg her to leave my father and come away to live with me, and though in those days I was little tempted to criticize her, I did frequently blame her in my own thoughts for timidity. I felt that she, on the one hand, and Father's family, on the other, were the two powers that were struggling for possession of my soul, and I hated every member of my father's family—even cousins I later grew fond of. It was not the people themselves I hated, of course, but drunkenness, dirt, and violence. I made an exception of my Uncle Laurence, because he was gentler than the others and had a sense of humour that partly qualified the O'Donovan gloom. When he was leaving for the front during the First World War, Grandmother, with her alcoholic emotionalism, began a beautiful scene that would have reduced poor Father to helpless sobs, but Laurence punctured it wickedly by pretending to sob even louder, and left Grandmother with the outraged expression that Shaw once versified as

> *Respect a mother's grief*
> *And give me time to finish out my scene.*

20

Child, I Know You're Going to Miss Me

Much as I pitied my aunt, I didn't really like her either; her affliction was never anything but terrible; and her wordless rages and griefs were as horrifying as those of a chained animal. But, like Mother, I was very fond of her husband, Pat Hanlon, because he was a man of great expressiveness and gaiety, and made his affliction serve his purposes. He was a wraith of a man with small black eyes and a little black moustache, and he lurched about in a curiously disjointed way, his head rolling from side to side. I think he hated the O'Donovan atmosphere as much as Mother did. He never joined in the drinking and was very industrious. When things became too difficult, he got down off the table on which he sat cross-legged, and lurched into our house with a snort and a shrug. Then he threw himself into a chair with that loose-jointed air of his and began describing his day in the Jewish tailor's in Patrick Street, his fingers flying, his small dark eyes flashing—really flashing—and queer animal noises that were intended to be laughter bubbling in his throat. He was a man who observed everything. I had never met the Jewish tailor, but he was as real to me as Charlie Chaplin, and just as funny. Hanlon was a superb mimic, and of everybody at once—the tailor, the customers, and the workgirls. Having no sound track to bother with, he acted at the speed of the earliest films, breaking off a scene or a part in an instant, impatiently grabbing and growling at Mother, who would be in hysterics, to tell her something new, though his thin face never lost its air of faint anxiety. At the end of a story he would give another shrug as a final commentary on the futility of human existence.

It was strange entertainment for a child, but I loved it—though, because I spoke slowly and only with my two hands, I often missed the point. Mother also

21

used her two hands, but she spoke fast and clearly and could understand Hanlon when he grew so excited that he fell back on one hand, and between hysterical fits of laughter she carried on a sort of subdued commentary to herself that told the story to Father and me. Then Hanlon would return to that dirty, uncomfortable house, having enjoyed a couple of hours of intelligent conversation with people far better equipped by nature than himself, and knowing that he had given at least as good as he got. And how many of us, with all our faculties, can feel as much when we leave someone's house? It was a real triumph of art over nature, and something it would take me twenty years to learn.

2

Father was a really fine-looking man. He was a six-footer and built to match, and years of work as a navvy had not affected the soldierly erectness of bearing he had picked up as a young man in the Army. He had a long Scandinavian head, but because of the slightly Mongolian cast of feature he had inherited from Grandmother, the lines of his face were horizontal instead of vertical. At the same time the bulge of the brows and the height of the cheekbones, instead of making his eyes seem weak, made them look as though they were twinkling. He was extraordinarily like certain photographs of the young Maxim Gorky. He dressed carefully, in the manner of an old-fashioned tradesman, in a blue serge suit with the cuffs of the trousers turned down over the heels, a bowler hat cocked a little to one side, and a starched shirt-front. Dressing him for Mass on Sunday was a serious task for any woman, for his fingers were all thumbs. He could rarely fasten his own studs, and it sometimes ended with his stamping and cursing before the big mirror, and Mother's grabbing at a stool to stand on, so that she could reach up to him, and begging him for the Lord's sake to keep quiet and let her do it for him. Then he put an open white handkerchief, casually disposed, in his breast pocket, and went down the road, graciously bowing and raising his hat to any woman he met, a fine figure of a man, and as vain as a child in his first sailor suit. In the "tall tales" he loved to tell of his soldiering days there was a great favourite of his about a review held by Queen Victoria during which she said: "And tell me, General, who is that distinguished-looking man in the second rank?" to which the general replied: "That, Your Majesty, is Michael O'Donovan, one of the best-looking men in your whole army."

Nothing could ever persuade Father that he was anything but a naturally home-loving body—which, indeed, for a great part of the time, he was. Nobody but himself could lock up the house for the night, and he had a big bolt for the back door and two bolts for the front, and only he could properly check the catch on the window, wind the alarm on the clock, and see that the lamp was out before we retired. Often he would be up first in the morning, give Mother a cup of tea in bed, and have a tremendous wash-up under the tap in the yard, winter and summer. Indeed, if there was snow he rubbed himself all over with it because it prevented chilblains. It was a bitter disappointment to him that I was a sissy, and he made angry comments when I drew a basin of water and then poured hot water from

24

the kettle into it. When he got in from work in the evening, he usually had a more leisurely, noisy wash, changed into old trousers and "slippers" that were old boots cut down and hacked in all directions so that the leather did not press on his corns, and, with his cap on to protect his head from drafts, sat at the head of the table by the window to read the evening *Echo* aloud to Mother, with comments that went on longer than the news. He began with the Police Court news to put him into good humour, and reserved for the last the political meetings, which made him scowl and mutter. "Oh, that unspeakable scut, George Crosbie!" I liked that till I began to read myself, but even then it did not disturb me much, for I was always too involved in what I read even to notice when neighbours dropped in.

This was just as well, because any project of Father's, from cutting his corns to writing to Whitehall about his pension, involved preparation on a major scale and something like general mobilization, and in any detail of this he could become entirely lost. For instance, when he wrote to Whitehall—this usually meant no more than filling out some form to show he was still alive—he had first of all to get the penny bottle of ink, and a new nib for the pen, and a bit of blotting-paper, and lay them all out on the table before him; then he had to get his papers, which were in a locked tin trunk in the bedroom, and he could never take one of these out without re-reading the lot: and on going through his discharge papers and discovering again what a model soldier he had been, he would be moved like an old novelist re-reading a review of his first talented book, and would have to bring them down and read them all over again to Mother, who knew them by heart. Every question on a questionnaire he read over several times before replying to it, because he knew it had been drafted by an old and cunning hand with the deliberate intention of catching him out. When he spotted the trap—and there nearly always was a trap—his whole face lit up with approval and he explained the problem carefully to Mother while he considered how best to handle it. He liked a subtle enemy because it enabled him to show how subtle he could be himself. He was a born hob-lawyer, always laying down the law about regulations, and greatly looked up to by other old soldiers, like Bill Heffernan, who were too humble even to pretend that they knew what the War Office wanted of them. When the form was filled out and in its envelope on the mantelpiece, and Mother had been warned that she must post it with her own hand and not entrust it to me, he would become emotional again about the goodness of the British Government and its consideration for its old servants—unlike the gnats of employers he worked for in Cork, who would see an old workman dying in the streets and not lift a hand to help him. The pension meant much more to him than the trifle of money it represented. It gave him a personal interest in the British Government. A Liberal Government might be good for the Irish cause, but a Conservative one would be better for the pension. It gave him wild dreams, because no quarter passed without his toying with the idea of compounding it for a capital sum, the size of which staggered imagination. It gave him the prospect of a happy old age, for when Mother died he could hand it in in return for provision in one of the military hospitals like Chelsea or Kilmainham where every day for the rest of his life he would get his pint of beer for nothing.

When the time came to cut his corns, he got a chair and rooted about on top of the wardrobe, which was his hidey-hole, well out of my reach, or intended to be; and after contemplating his many treasures, he took down his current razor, wrapped in oiled cloth, and a couple of other, older razors that he had either abandoned or picked up from those who had no further use for them but that could be trusted to do the rough work of corn-cutting. Then he got the wash-basin, and a jug of cold water, and a kettle of boiling water, and a bottle of corn cure, and a paper of some sort to read while his feet soaked, and a hand mirror to see the parts of his feet that were normally hard to see, and anything else that could conceivably be of use to him, and then, with Mother or myself lined up to hold the mirror, he was set for the evening. Not that I ever remember his doing it without cutting himself.

Or else it was an evening with his pipes. He was an inveterate magpie, and everything that anyone else threw away Father would pick up, in the full conviction that if you kept it for seven years it would be bound to come in useful, while the person who had discarded it would probably pay for his improvidence by dying in the workhouse. Old broken pipes were a tremendous temptation to him, and he had a large collection of bowls and stems, all of which needed only careful handling to turn them into brand-new pipes of the most expensive kind. This task would have been considerably easier if he had ever had anything like a gimlet handy, but as he rarely did, he had to make a tool. Usually, the treasure chest yielded some sort of blade, and some sort of handle, and the blade had to be heated and set in the handle, and then the handle usually burst and had to be bound with a bit of string or wax-end. Then the improvised tool had to be heated again, and the bowl or the stem burned till the two pieces could be joined. I can still remember the rancid smell of burned amber. The result was usually most

peculiar—a delicate bowl joined to a colossal stem or a
delicate stem to a rural bowl—but Father puffed it
with great satisfaction, in the belief that he had cheated
some ruffian of a tobacco merchant out of the price of
a brand-new pipe.

Father was, I think, a naturally melancholy man;
though he was always pleased when people called, he
rarely called on anybody himself; and, like all melancholy men, he made his home his cave, and devoted a
great deal of thought to its beauty and utility. Unfortunately, he was one of the most awkward men who
ever handled a tool, and it is a subject I can speak on
with some authority, for I have inherited his awkwardness. Along with the razors, the pipe bowls and stems
and the rest, he had a peculiar hoard of tools and
equipment, mostly stored on top of the wardrobe. They
had been lovingly accumulated over the years in the
conviction that eventually they would be bound to
come in useful. Prior to tackling any major job, all
this had to be unloaded onto the kitchen table, and
Father put on his glasses and studied it affectionately
in the way in which he studied the documents in the
tin trunk, forgetting whatever he was supposed to be
looking for as he recited the history of hinges, bolts,
screws, wooden handles, blades, clock springs, and
mysterious-looking bits of machinery that had probably
fallen out of a railway engine in process of dissolution,
and wondered what some of them could be used for.

Finally, having selected his equipment—the nice
bit of timber that would nearly do for a shelf, and the
brackets that didn't quite match, and the screws or
nails that were either a bit too long or a bit too short,
and the old chisel that would do for a screw-driver, and
the hammer with the loose head—Father set to work.
He had lined up my mother and myself as builder's

mates, to hold the plank and the hammer, the saw that needed setting, and the nails and screws. Before he had been at work for five minutes, the top of the hammer would have flown off and hit him in the face, or the saw would have cut the chair instead of the plank, or the nail that was to have provided the setting for the screw would have carried away inches of the plank with the unmerciful wallops he gave it. Father had the secret of making inanimate objects appear to possess a secret, malevolent life of their own, and sometimes it was hard to believe that his tools and materials were not really in a conspiracy against him.

His first reaction to this behaviour was chagrin that, for all his love and care, they were turning on him again, but this soon changed to blind rage and an autocratic determination to put them in their places. Hacking away great chunks of the plaster, he nailed in the brackets any old way, while Mother and I, our hearts in our mouths, stood by with anything we thought might come in handy. He swore bloody murder, exactly as he did when the studs in his shirt-front turned against him before Mass on Sunday and it became a toss-up whether, to spite them, he might not go to Mass at all; and in the same gentle voice Mother besought him to let it alone and not to be upsetting himself like that. And when it was all over, and the kitchen a wreck, he would sit down with gloomy pride to read a paper he could not concentrate on, obsessed by the image of himself as a good man and kind father on whom everybody and everything turned.

That was why, in spite of the fact that he had a cobbler's last among his treasures, and that I was forever hacking the good boots that were bought for me with his money, he didn't often try his hand at cobbling. A man who could hardly hit a three-inch nail with a large hammer could not be expected to do much with a shoemaker's tack. Most often it was Mother who did the cobbling, buying a patch or a pair of half-soles in town and tacking them on herself. But I seem to remember that his hoarding instinct betrayed him once when he discovered a large strip of fan-belting from a factory, made of some extraordinary material which he maintained was stronger than leather and would save us a fortune, and he did cut strips off this and nail them to his working boots, on which they looked like pieces of board. On the other hand, he liked rough tailoring, and was perfectly happy sewing a patch onto his working trousers.

But I never minded Father as a handyman the way I minded him as a barber. He always had one pair of clippers, and sometimes two, wrapped in oily rags among the other treasures, and, according to him, these clippers had saved him untold expense. Given a pencil and paper, he could even work it out, as he worked out the amount he saved by being a teetotaller. He was a great man for saving. "My couple of ha'pence," he used to call it. Mother, I suspect, never knew how much he really earned, and when he was sober he usually had a substantial sum in the locked trunk in the bedroom. When he was feeling depressed, he went upstairs by way of consulting his documents and counted it softly, but not so softly that we couldn't hear the chink of the coins as he caressed them. He was a bit of a skinflint and disliked the improvident way Mother bought me sweets, biscuits, or boys' weeklies, not to mention toys at Christmas—a season that seemed to have been specially invented for his mortification. Father, of course, was only providing for the rainy day.

So, on a sunny afternoon, he would take down the

clippers, pull off the oily rags, adjust the blades, set a chair in the back yard, and, with a towel round his neck, let Mother cut his hair. There was no great difficulty about this, since all Father wanted was the equivalent of a close shave. According to him, this was excellent for the growth of the hair, and one of his ambitions was to double his savings by protecting my hair as well. I didn't want my hair protected, though he assured me angrily that I would be bald before I was grown up at all; neither did Mother want it, and so, the moment it grew a bit too long and she saw Father casting brooding glances at it, she gave me tuppence to go to the barber. This made Father furious, for not only had she again demonstrated her fundamental improvidence, but Curtin, the barber, would have left me with what Father called "a most unsightly mop." It was like the business of wanting me to wash under the tap. But no matter how carefully she watched over me, he sometimes caught me with the clippers in his hand, and I had to sit on a chair in the back yard, sobbing and sniffling, while he got to work on me and turned me into a laughing-stock for the neighbourhood. He went about it in exactly the same way that he went about cutting his corns or putting up a shelf. "Wisha, is it the way you want to make the child look like a convict?" Mother would cry indignantly, and Father would stamp and curse and pull at a whole chunk of hair till I screamed, and then curse again and shout: "It's your own fault, you little puppy, you! Why can't you stop quiet?"

Then one evening Father would be late, and Mother and I would sit over the fire, half crazy with panic, and I would say prayers to the Sacred Heart and the Blessed Virgin to look after him. I can never remember that my prayers had any effect. Finally, he would come in, full of fallacious good humour, and stand at the door, rubbing his palms and puckering up his lips in a sly grin. He expressed great—indeed, undue—surprise at the lateness of the hour. He had been detained talking to a man he hadn't met for fifteen years—not since the funeral of poor Jack Murphy of the Connaught Rangers in September '98, which he remembered distinctly because Tim O'Connor, God rest him, had been there as well, and the three of them had left the funeral together and spent the evening in a pub called Keohane's that used to be at the corner of Windmill Road but had since been torn down. He would ramble on like that for half an hour, in loosely related clauses that gave the impression of coherence but were difficult to follow, and toward ten o'clock would decide to take a little stroll. That was the end of Father in his role as a home-loving body. Next evening he would slink upstairs to the locked trunk where he kept his savings, and then go out again. The rainy day had at last arrived. He would return in a state of noisy amiability that turned to sullenness when it failed to rouse a response. I was most often to blame for this because, in spite of Mother's appeals to me not to answer him back, I could not bear his maudlin attentions, which made him so like my grandmother, and, like her, he was offended, and snarled that I was "better fed than taught." The day after, he would not go to work and at twelve or one would be at the trunk again and off for a longer carouse.

The savings usually lasted him for a week or ten days. When they were exhausted, Mother had to go to the pawnshop with his best blue suit. So that the neighbours would not see what she was doing, she would put on her long black shawl. I hated the very sight of that shawl, even though I knew that it suited her long, thin, virginal face; it meant an immediate descent in the social scale from the "hatties" to the "shawlies"— the poorest of the poor. I also hated the pawning of the blue suit, because it meant that Father stopped going for walks or to Mass—especially to Mass, for he would not have dreamed of worshipping God in anything less dignified than blue serge—and it meant that we had him all day about the house, his head swollen, his eyes bloodshot, sitting by the fire and shivering in the fever of alcoholism or getting up and walking to and fro, unable to read, unable to work, unable to think of anything except drink. Home was no longer a refuge for him. It had become a prison and a cage, and the only hope of escaping from it was more money. When Mother returned from town and put the five or six shillings on the table with the pawn tickets, he sometimes turned on her with an angry "Lord God, was that all you got on it?" It was not so much that he expected more as that staging a quarrel at this point meant that she would not dare to ask him for money for food, or the rent, or the insurance, or Levin the peddler, who had sold her a suit for me.

Two days later she would be off again with one of the two clocks—her own clock from the bedroom, which did not have an alarm. After that came the clock with the alarm, which was no longer necessary as he did not go to work, and then his silver watch. "In God's name, Mick Donovan, do you want to put us on the street?" she would cry, and he would stamp and shout like a madman. He didn't know what being put on the street meant as she, the orphan, did. Then her blue costume went, and his military medals, and, lastly, his "ring paper"—so called because it was printed in a series of small circles intended for the post-office date stamp—his authority for drawing his Army pension.

Though the transaction was illegal, the security was excellent. Even then he would be greedily eying the wedding ring on her finger and whining at her to pawn this as well, "just for a couple of days till I steady up," but it was only when she was really desperate that she let this go, and it took precedence of everything else when the time came to reclaim the little bits of married life. By this time all the money coming into the house would be the ninepence or shilling she earned as a charwoman, and he would be striding like a caged tiger up and down the kitchen in the dusk, waiting for her to come in from work so that he could get this from her.

"Come on!" he would say with forced joviality. "Tuppence is all I want. Me entrance fee!"

"And where am I to get the child's dinner?" she would cry in despair. "Or is it the way you want us to starve?"

"Look, it's all over now. No one is going to starve. Can't you see I'm steadying up? Come on, woman, give us the money!"

"Stay here, then, and I'll go and get it for you!"

"I don't want you to get it for me," he would say, turning nasty. "Getting it for him" was a later stage, which occurred only when he had completely exhausted his credit and old friends cleared out when he came red-eyed and fighting mad into the pub. With his "entrance fee," as he called it, he had not only the price of a drink but the chance of cadging more, either from the barmaid, if the publican was out, or from one of his old cronies.

If he did not get the money immediately, his tone would change again and he would become whining and maudlin. As night came on and his chances of a real debauch diminished, he would grow vicious. "Jesus

34

Christ, I'll put an end to this!" he would mutter, and take down his razor. His threats were never empty, as I well knew since the night when I was an infant and he flung the two of us out into Blarney Lane in our night clothes, and we shivered there in the roadway till some neighbours took us in and let us lie in blankets before the fire. Whenever he brandished the razor at Mother, I went into hysterics, and a couple of times I threw myself on him, beating him with my fists. That drove her into hysterics, too, because she knew that at times like that he would as soon have slashed me as her. Later, in adolescence, I developed pseudo-epileptic fits that were merely an externalization of this recurring nightmare, and though I knew they were not real, and was ashamed of myself for indulging in them at all, I could not resist them when once I had yielded to the first nervous spasm.

In those days, the house would be a horror. Only when he had money for drink would we have peace for an hour, and sometimes Mother borrowed it just to get him out of the house. When I was old enough to go to school, I would come back at three o'clock and scout round to make sure that he was not at home. If he wasn't, I would sneak in and hastily make myself a cup of tea. If he was, I did without the tea and wandered round the rest of the afternoon, waiting till it was time to intercept Mother on her way home from work. I never went near my grandmother. From the moment Father began his drinking bout, you could feel her disapproval of Mother and me—the two heartless creatures who did not sympathize with her darling son. This, she seemed to say, all came of Father's mistake in marrying a woman who did not know her place, a would-be lady. When I talked of him to Mother, I always called him "he" or "him," carefully eschewing the

name of "Father" which would have seemed like profa-
nation to me. "You must not speak like that of your father, child," Mother would say severely. "Whatever he
does, he's still your father." I resented her loyalty to
him. I wanted her to talk to me about him the way I
knew the neighbours talked. They could not understand why she did not leave him. I realize now that to
do so she would have had to take a job as housekeeper
and put me into an orphanage—the one thing in the
world that the orphan child could not do.

It always ended in the same way—only when we
were completely destitute; when the shop-keepers refused Mother even a loaf of bread, and the landlord
threatened us with eviction, and Father could no
longer raise the price of a single pint. At that point only
did he give in—"cave in" better describes what really
happened to him. Sour and savage and silent, he began to look for another job. He rarely went back to the
job he had left, and in those days I believed it was because he had lost it. Now I am certain that he was far
too good a workman to be put off because of a drinking
bout, however prolonged, and that he was too humiliated to go back. To have done that would have been to
admit his weakness and guilt. He was, as I have said,
a proud man, and he would never have admitted to the
other poor labourers, whom he despised, that he had
sunk so low. And because something had to be done
about the mass of debt that had accumulated in the
meantime, he and Mother would have to go to the loan
office in Paul Street, accompanied by some friend to
act as guarantor. Mother had to go with him, because
even at this stage he would still have taken the money
and drunk it along with the rest. I was very impressed
by the big interest we had to pay, and it struck me
that if only I could accumulate a little capital and lend

36

them the money myself, it would be an excellent way both of getting rich and of saving Mother anxiety— the money would, at least, be in the family. But my own savings usually evaporated in the first few days of strain, and I realized that I would need a more settled background before I could set up in business as a money-lender.

With the aid of the loan, Father would take out his "ring paper" and draw his pension, and out of that he would release his best suit, so that he could again worship God on Sundays in the Dominican Church on the Sand Quay. Then would come the clocks and the watch and chain and the military medals, and finally Mother's blue costume. It was characteristic of him that when he started to put money aside again, it was to pay the publicans. He preferred to let Mother work for a shilling a day rather than defer the payment of his drinking debts. It would seem to be obvious that he was only preparing the way for another debauch—because this, in fact, was the ultimate effect of it—and yet I should still say that this was untrue. I am sure it was pride that moved him. I don't think Mother had much pride. Gay people have no need of pride because gaiety is merely the outward sign of inward integrity, but Father had no integrity; as with all mentally sick people, the two sides of his nature hardly communicated and were held together by pins and Hail Marys, and pride was one of the ways in which he protected the false conception of his own character that was one side.

And once again the little house was reconstituted about that incomplete conception of Father as a home-loving body, and a new cycle began. Brisk and cheerful, he rose in the early morning to wash under the tap and bring Mother a cup of tea in bed, and in the evenings he read the *Echo* to her while I sat in some corner, absorbed in my own boys' weekly, and a wind blew up the river and seemed to isolate us as on a ship at sea. On such evenings, no one could doubt his love for her or hers for him, but I, who had no other security, knew better than she did what he was really like, and watched him suspiciously, in the way that only a child can watch, and felt that all authority was only a pretense and that God Himself was probably not much better, and directed my prayers not to Him, but to His mother, who had said nothing but merely suffered.

Because I was jealous of him, I knew that there was real devotion between that strangely assorted pair, and yet I often wonder what really went on in Mother's mind during those terrible years. I think when she wasn't entirely desperate, pity was what was uppermost in her mind, pity for this giant of a man who had no more self-knowledge or self-control than a baby. The least pain could bewilder and madden him and even a toothache could drive him to drink. He died as he had lived, wandering about Cork, looking for drink when he was in the last stages of pneumonia, and I, who might have controlled him, was not informed because it would upset me too much, and besides Mother felt I wouldn't understand. Even God wouldn't understand. Whenever his anniversary came round, she withdrew into herself for weeks, and, without a word to anyone, the offering for Masses was sent to the Cistercians at Mount Melleray, because God might fail to realize that poor Father really was at heart a home-loving body and a good husband and father, and might keep him too long in Purgatory, a place he would not be happy in at all because he could not stand pain, and even a toothache would drive him mad.

Once only did she say anything significant, and

38

that was while she was raving. I was a grown man and living in Dublin, and I came back to Cork on holiday to find her desperately ill, and poor Father—the world's most hopeless man with his hands—devotedly nursing her with nothing but neat whisky. I blasted him for not wiring for me, and he snarled back: "How could I, when she wouldn't let me?" And then he sat over the fire, flapping his hands and snivelling: "What would I do without her?" When I had made her comfortable for the night, I sat with her, holding her hand, and heard her muttering about me as though I were not there.

"God! God!" she whispered. "He raised me from the gutter where the world threw me. He raised me from the gutter where the world threw me!"

3

WHENEVER I READ about juvenile delin-
quents, I find myself thinking of Mother,
because she was whatever the opposite of a juvenile
delinquent is, and this was not due to her upbringing
in a Catholic orphanage, since whatever it was in her
that was the opposite of a juvenile delinquent was too
strong to have been due to the effect of any environment, and, indeed, resisted a number of environments
to which no reasonable person would subject a child;
the gutter where life had thrown her was deep and
dirty. One way of describing this quality is to call it
gaiety; another is to say that she was a woman who
passionately believed in the world of appearances. If
something appeared to be so, or if she had been told
it was so, then she believed it to be so. This, as every
psychologist knows, leads to disillusionments, and

when a juvenile delinquent is disillusioned we describe it as a traumatic experience. So far as I could see, up to her death practically all Mother's experiences were traumatic, including, I am afraid, her experience with me. And some small portion of her simple-mindedness she did pass on to me.

She was small and dainty, with long dark hair that she was very proud of. She had only two faults that I ever knew of—she was vain and she was obstinate— and the fact that these qualities were masked by humility and gentleness prevented my recognizing them till I was a grown man. Father, who was as grey as a badger at thirty-five, and in danger of growing bald, in spite of his clippers, was very jealous of her beautiful dark hair, and whenever he wanted to make her mad he would affect to discover white strands in it. Being an orphan, she had no notion of her own age, and had never known a birthday, but Father had discussed it with my Uncle Tim and satisfied himself that she was several years older than himself. When he believed she was seventy, he got really angry because he was sure she was going to let her vanity deprive her of a perfectly good pension. Mother shrugged this off as another example of his jealousy. To tell the truth, that was what I thought myself. She looked, at the time, like a well-preserved fifty-five. However, to put his mind at rest, I had the date of her birth looked up in the Customs House in Dublin, and discovered that she was only a few months short of seventy. Father was triumphant, but I felt guilty because I feared that the knowledge of her real age would make her become old. I needn't have worried. I think she probably decided finally that though the Registrar of Births and Deaths was a well-intentioned man, he was not particularly bright.

She had a lordly way with any sort of record she could get her hands on that conflicted with her own view of herself—she merely tore it up. Once, the poet George Russell did a charming pencil drawing of her, which I had framed. The next time I came home on holiday, I found the frame filled with snapshots of me, and my heart sank, because I knew what must have happened. "What did you do with that drawing?" I asked, hoping she might at least have preserved it, and she replied firmly: "Now, I'm just as fond of AE as you are, but I could not have that picture round the house. He made me look like a poisoner." When she was eighty-five, and we were leaving to live in England, I discovered that she had done the same thing with the photograph in her passport. She was entirely unaffected by my anger. "The sergeant of the police at Saint Luke's said it," she proclaimed firmly. "The man who took that picture should be tried for his life." I think she was glad to have official authority for her personal view that I had been very remiss in not bringing proceedings against the photographer. When my wife and I separated, the only indication I had of Mother's feelings was when I looked at my photograph album one day and saw that every single photograph of my wife had been destroyed. Where she had been photographed with me or the children her picture had been cut away. It was not all malice, any more than the destruction of her own pictures was all vanity. I am certain it went back to some childish technique of endurance by obliterating impressions she had found too terrible to entertain, as though, believing as she did in the world of appearances, she found it necessary to alter the world of appearances to make it seem right, but in time it came to affect almost everything she did. It even worked in reverse, for one Christmas an old friend, Stan Stewart, sent her a book, but because it came straight from his bookseller, it did not contain an inscription, as books that were sent to me did. After her death, I found the book with a charming inscription from Stan, written in by herself. Her affection for him made her give herself away, for she wrote "From dear Stan."

She was beautiful, and—in later life at least—she knew it. Once a well-known woman writer came to the house, and when she was introduced to Mother, she threw her arms about her neck and hugged her. "But she's so beautiful!" she said to me later in apology, and Mother accepted the tribute modestly as indicating that our visitor showed nice feelings. She had a long, pale, eager face that lit up as though there had been an electric torch behind it, and whenever people told her anything interesting, she studied their faces with a delighted or grieved expression. It was part of her belief in the reality of the objective world. She knew that when people were happy they laughed, and she laughed with them—not so much at what they said, because sometimes she didn't understand what they were saying, as in sympathy with their happiness. In the same way, when they were sad she looked grieved. It never occurred to her that people could be happy and wear a mournful face. From her point of view, this would have been a mere waste of good happiness. For the same reason, she never teased and could never understand teasing, which was the amusement of people like Father, who do not believe in the world of appearances, and though she was clever and sometimes profound, she went through life burdened with the most extraordinary misapprehensions, which she clung to with gentle persistence.

When I was a child, our walks often took us to the Good Shepherd Convent, in the orphanage of which she had grown up. I liked it because it had trees and steep lawns and pleasant avenues. On fine days we sat with one of her old friends on the lawn that overlooked the valley of the river, or, on showery ones, in the grotto of the nuns' cemetery, and Mother of Perpetual Succour, who was in charge of the garden, took me round and picked me fruit, and I suspect that sometimes, when things were not going well at home, Mother Blessed Margaret gave Mother small gifts of money and clothes. In the convent cemetery, among the tiny crosses of the nuns, was a big monument to one of the orphans, an infant known as Little Nellie of Holy God, who had suffered and died in a particularly edifying way, and about whom, at the time, a certain cult was growing up. I had a deep personal interest in her, because not only was I rather in that line myself, but Father had assisted at her exhumation when her body was removed from a city cemetery, and verified the story that it was perfectly preserved. Having attended several funerals, seen the broken coffins and the bones that were heaped on the side, and heard my relatives say knowingly: "That was Eugene now. The one below him was Mary," I was strongly in favour of the saintly life. When they dug me up, I wanted to be intact.

But much as I enjoyed the elegance of the convent gardens and avenues, it was there that I picked up the fragments of Mother's past life that have never ceased to haunt me. At that time, of course, they were merely a few hints, but they were sufficient to sustain my interest through the years, and later I wrote down and got her to write down as many of the facts as she remembered—or cared to remember. I stopped doing this one day when she put down her pen with a look of horror and said: "I can't write any more—it's too terrible!"

It was. She had been the oldest of four children

whose parents lived in a tiny cabin at the top of Blarney Lane beyond the point where I grew up. After her had come Margaret, then Tim, and then Nora, the baby. My grandmother was a country girl from Donoughmore, and had been married in the hood cloak, the traditional dress of country women of her day. My grandfather was a labourer in Arnott's Brewery, which was near St. Mary's of the Isle Convent, at the other side of the city. Mother was his pet, and sometimes when he went to work he carried her with him in his arms, left her in the playground of the convent to amuse herself, and then came back later to carry her home again. He was a powerful man, a bowls player and athlete, and one day, for a bet, he began lifting heavy casks and injured his back. While he was in the Mercy Hospital Mother was not allowed to visit him—I fancy because my grandmother had to work and Mother looked after the children—and, being his pet, she resented it. One day she left the children behind and ran all the way down Sunday's Well and Wyse's Hill and across the old wooden bridge where St. Vincent's Bridge now stands to the hospital. She found him, fully dressed, sitting on his bed in the men's ward upstairs, with a group of men about him who played with her and gave her sweets. When she was leaving he came down the stairs with her, and at the front door, asked if she knew her way home. She said that she did, but he realized that she was confused, caught her up in his arms and made off with her for home. Mother told that part of the story in a rather tentative way, and I suspect that, with a child's belief in magic, she had always felt that her visit had cured him, and could not face the possibility that it might have been the cause of his death. Anyhow, I doubt if it was. I think he knew he was dying, and wanted to die at home. He lingered only a short while, and Mother remembered how he reported the stages of dying to my grandmother. "The end is coming, Julia," he said once. "The hearing is going on me now."

After his death, neighbours and friends took the children in. My grandmother's people in Donoughmore, who were comfortably off, refused to do anything for her. Nora, taken by one couple, was never heard of again in this world, though in later years Mother tried hard to track her down. Someone else took Tim. Margaret, I fancy, remained on with Grandmother. Mother fell to the lot of a foreman in the Brewery named O'Regan, who lived with his childless wife in a place called Brandy Lane on the south side of the city. They were a good-natured couple, but with no comprehension of a child's needs. After the intimacy of the little cabin, Mother was terrified of her own tall solitary bedroom and the street-lamp outside that threw its light up onto the ceiling, and in the daytime Mrs. O'Regan went out and left her alone in the house. One day she dragged a chair into the hall and managed to lift the latch. Then she ran wild through the city streets till a policeman picked her up and brought her home by the hand.

It was only a brief respite, because a couple of days later they were evicted for not paying the rent, and Mother and Margaret sat for hours on the roadside with the remains of their little home: the tester bed, the picture of Sir John Arnott, the brewer, and the picture of the Guardian Angel—the two protectors who had done so little for them. After that, Grandmother took Mother and Margaret to the Good Shepherd Orphanage, and when Mother realized that they were being left behind, she rushed after my grandmother, clinging to her skirts and screaming to be taken home. My grandmother's whispered reply is one of the phrases that haunted my childhood—indeed, it haunts me still. "But, my store, I have no home now." For me, there has always been in imagination a stage beyond death —a stage where one says "I have no home now."

My grandmother went mad under the strain and was for a time in the Lunatic Asylum. When she came out, she worked for a few months as a maid. She used to visit Mother and Aunt Margaret at the orphanage, and once she brought Tim, then two, who was on his way to an infants' orphanage in Waterford. To begin with, the two little girls were comfortable enough. They were too young to dress themselves, so they were dispensed from the necessity for going to Mass, and for the same reason they didn't attend classes and were left in the kitchen with the older girls who did the cooking. Their cots were side by side in the dormitory, and sometimes Mother got into Margaret's bed and was caught there at 6.30 when Mother Cecilia came into the dormitory, clapping her hands and reciting the morning offering.

By the time Mother was attending classes, fever broke out in the school and a temporary hospital had to be erected in the grounds. Margaret disappeared with many of the others, but by this time Mother was growing used to disappearances. One day two girls entered the classroom, carrying a third whose legs dragged dead behind her.

"Minnie," they said. "Here's your sister."

Mother ran away, and then the tall, thin girl they were carrying began to cry. Margaret was now a cripple for life and lived in the infirmary. It was Mother who carried her to and from the classrooms, where she could move about fairly well by swinging on the desks. She had developed into something of a pet and a tyrant. She was precocious, and read everything that came her

47

way. Whatever poetry she read, she immediately memorized. She developed a hatred of injustice, and attacked even the nuns when she thought they were
doing wrong. She despised Mother's timidity, and when
Mother peered in the infirmary door to see if any nuns
were round, Margaret called out to her not to be such
a coward. The owner of the Queen's Old Castle, one of
the big city stores, who sometimes visited the convent,
had a wheel-chair made for her so that she could be
pushed round.

When Grandmother was dying in the workhouse,
only Mother could make the journey to say good-bye to
her. Grandmother wept, and Mother took out her own
handkerchief to dry her tears. As she left the workhouse, she remembered the handkerchief. It was school
property, and she might be punished for the loss of it,
so she rushed back to the ward. Grandmother was still
weeping, but Mother could not keep the lay sister waiting in the convent cab.

Grandmother's gentleness and humility had endeared her to some of the nuns, and when she died,
Reverend Mother decided to save her from what was
considered the shame of the paupers' hole, where the
unclaimed bodies of the dead were thrown. Mother
Mary Magdalen was a lady, and did not allow the other
nuns to forget it. Her family had been of Isaac Butt's
party, as opposed to the popular party of Parnell. "My
brothers were in Parliament when there were none but
gentlemen there," she told the children. She also told
them that she had found her vocation at the age of
twenty-eight, while attending a performance of *The
Colleen Bawn* at the Opera House in Cork. I wonder
whether the subject of the play, which deals with the
seduction of an innocent Irish girl, and her peculiar
choice of a name in religion do not imply that she

considered herself to have been flighty. She sent for
Mother to find out where Grandfather was buried, but
Mother did not know. So Grandmother was buried in a
city graveyard, and Reverend Mother ordered a hearse
and two covered cars—the old-fashioned two-wheeled
vehicles known only in Cork. In one rode Mother with a
lay sister, and in the other a couple of the orphans.

There was little of the agony of the orphan child
that Mother did not know, either through her own experience or the experiences of the other children,
which she observed in her sympathetic way. It was the
height of the Land War, and all over Ireland poor cot-
tagers were being thrown on to the roadside by police
and British troops. One frightened little girl went about
for days asking: "Will the men with the wed wousers
(red trousers) come here too?" Once, a baby girl called
Lynch, from Kerry, whose family had been drowned
was missing for hours, and was finally discovered in
the empty chapel, patiently knocking on the altar and
calling: "Holy God! Holy God! Are 'oo there? Will 'oo
send up my Dadda?" Some of the children did not realize for days the immensity of the change that had
come over their lives. For a whole week one little girl
called Anne Dorgan patiently watched the clock till it
came to half past three and then stood up and raised
her hand, asking meekly: "Please, ma'am, can I go
home now?" "Sit down, Anne Dorgan," the nun would
say gently, but Anne would stick to her point. "But,
ma'am, 'tis half past three. 'Tis time to go home,
ma'am."

In time she too realized as Mother had done that
she had no home now, and tried to divert her feeling
for home to the convent and for her parents to some
nun. In some girls that switch was never affected at
all and they remained to the end of their lives aloof

and cold and conscious of some lack of warmth in themselves, like Kate Gaynor, a friend of Mother's whom I knew in later years and who said bitterly that every orphanage in the world should be torn down because they robbed a child of natural affection, but others were luckier or maybe less exacting. Mother used to quote a snatch of conversation that she had overheard between two infants sitting on the ground under a window, the one eager and serious, the other bored and pompous.

"Do you love God?"

"I won't tell you."

"Do you love Mother Saint Paul?"

"I won't tell you."

"Do you rather God or Mother Saint Paul?"

"I won't tell you."

"I think I rather God, and then Mother Saint Paul."

Then there was silence. Perhaps the child who would not tell was one whose natural affection was being killed.

Mother herself did not see my Uncle Tim for five years, and in the meantime he had been transferred to the Boys' Orphanage at Greenmount on the south side of the river. On her feast day, Reverend Mother decided that girls who had brothers there should be allowed to entertain them in Sunday's Well. Mother was now quite an important person, and she allowed one of her friends to join her in collecting candies and biscuits for the expected visit. My Aunt Margaret in the infirmary had a hoard. When the orphan boys marched up the convent avenue behind their band, Mother and her friend ran screaming through the ranks calling "O'Connor! Tim O'Connor!" A small boy said modestly "That's me," and the two little girls stuffed his pockets with sweets and marched him off in triumph to the infirmary. But another little girl, called Eileen O'Connor, rushed after them weeping and crying that they had stolen her brother. When they realized their mistake, Mother and her friend beat the pretender and took back the sweets before returning to look for the real Tim O'Connor. After that, the experiment of allowing brothers and sisters to meet for one afternoon in the year was not repeated.

Meanwhile, Mother had her living to earn. She had been trained as a bookbinder, and was neat and skilful at this, as she was at almost anything she tackled, but she was always getting into trouble for reading the books she should have been binding. Maria Condon, who was in charge of the bookbinding class and was a gentle, grave, responsible girl, used to smile sadly and shake her head over Mother's tendency to be distracted by printed pages. She was the daughter of one of the "fallen" women in the penitentiary and was allowed to see her mother once a week in a convent parlour. One of Mother Mary Magdalen's reforms had been to make a clean sweep of illegitimate girls from the school on the plea that it was unfair to the orphans to have an additional presumption of illegitimacy against them, but an exception had been made of Maria because her mother, who had been seduced by a well-known doctor, had taken vows and become what was known as a "dedicated penitent," serving a life term by choice in atonement for her fall. There was a moving sequel to the story of Maria and her mother which disturbed me greatly when I was an adolescent and caused endless argument between Mother and myself.

When Maria was sixteen or seventeen she had to be sent out to work as a maid, but the nuns decided that it was unsafe for her to work in Ireland, where people would get to know of her illegitimacy. Maria, who had been told nothing about this, wanted to remain in Cork, where she could be close to her mother, but instead the nuns sent her to New York as maid in a rough Irish boarding house. An older girl who was also a maid in New York was told to look after her. Maria was homesick; she wanted to save her wages to earn her fare back to Ireland, and finally the older girl told her why she could not go back. Maria returned to the horrible boarding house, packed her few possessions, and was not heard of again for a long time. She had been so horrified at her mother's "sin" and her own illegitimacy that she had decided to break off all connection with her mother and the convent.

After the revelation, she had gone out and taken the first job she was offered. Fortunately for her, this was with an old American family who soon realized that she was a superior and intelligent girl. But they could not understand why she never received or wrote letters. Finally, the mistress of the house questioned her, and Maria, believing that since she was illegitimate she would be dismissed, broke down and told her everything. Her employers were shocked, and they insisted on her writing at once to her mother. Correspondence with her was resumed, but the nuns were hostile —Maria had left the good Catholic home they had found for her. Her employers encouraged Maria to get a better job and save for a little home of her own to which she could bring her mother. When she had saved enough she returned to Cork, but she found the nuns openly hostile to her plans, and her mother refused to go back with her. She had taken her vows and would end her days as an unpaid trusty in a penitentiary.

As was only natural, when I learned the truth about Maria, I had no sympathy for anyone but her, but Mother refused to let me criticize the nuns. "They did what they thought was right," she said obstinately and that settled it for her. But it didn't settle it for me, and I have never ceased to be haunted by the images of Maria and her mother, whose innocent lives had been blasted by an introverted religion.

Mother must have been a dreamy, sensitive child, because she had spells of somnambulism, and once she was found walking up and down a convent corridor in her nightdress, reciting Wolsey's speech from *Henry VIII*—"Farewell, a long farewell, to all my greatness!"

She was not sent to a bookbinder's to work. One winter evening, when she was fourteen or fifteen, the Mistress of Studies came to her in the orphanage workroom where she was sewing and told her she had found a nice home for her with two ladies who had called to enquire for a maid. The Mistress of Studies then went out and returned with a regular convent outfit for girls who were leaving school—a black straw sailor hat and black coat, a pair of gloves, and a parcel of clean aprons. Mother gathered up her own possessions—a statue of the Blessed Virgin and a couple of holy pictures—said good-bye to her friends, and went off in the darkness down Sunday's Well in a covered car with the two ladies, a Mrs. Bowen, who was a widow, and her daughter-in-law. The car stopped outside a terrace of new two-storey houses on Gardiner's Hill.

Mother thought the Mistress of Studies had probably been mistaken, because it didn't seem a very good home. The younger of the two women lit a candle and showed her her room, which was a little cubbyhole with a fireplace, a bed, and two or three framed Bible texts. Mother unpacked her belongings and ranged the statue of the Blessed Virgin and the holy pictures on the mantelpiece to keep her company. After her tea she sat in the kitchen till Mrs. Bowen told her it was time for her to go to bed. Then she lit her candle and went up to her room. That night all her old fears came back. Since she had been taken by the O'Regans she had never slept alone in a room. She had become used to the big classrooms and dormitories, the voices and the loud footsteps along the corridors, and she was terrified. When she left her room, she stooped for fear of knocking her head on the lintel, which was so much lower than in the big doorways she was used to, and dreaded to move lest she knock something over.

The Bowens were poor, and Mother got no wages, but the younger woman was a dressmaker, and made Mother some clothes of her own, which she liked just as well. Anyhow, she was not accustomed to money. (One of the orphans had once stolen a pound and gone straight to a sweet store, where she ordered "a pound's worth of sweets"—as though a child of our own time should ask for twenty dollars' worth of candies.) The Bowens kept two lodgers, and the younger woman waited on them. She was an eager, earnest housekeeper, forever on the rush, and so careful of the scraps that she sometimes kept bread till it turned green. Once, Mother was throwing it out, but Mrs. Bowen gave her a lecture on waste and explained that bread was healthier that way. Being a great believer in the world of appearances, Mother tried to like it, but couldn't. She decided that, like the view that the Mistress of Studies held of the Bowens' house, this was just a mistake.

Mr. Bowen had a job in a wine store on Merchant's Quay, but his health was poor, and Mother was frequently sent into town to explain his absences. She was very sorry about his bad health, but she enjoyed the trips into town. At nights she was allowed to read in the parlour while the Bowens sang sentimental or comic songs, or, on Sunday, hymns—Protestant hymns of course. Mother's own favourites were always the old Latin hymns like "Ave Maris Stella" and "Stabat Mater," but she thoroughly enjoyed the Protestant ones, having, like her son, an open mind on the subject of anything with a tune. The books at her disposal were limited in appeal, boy's school stories with a strongly sectarian bias and standard editions of the poets, but at least she was able to read Shakespeare right through.

When she was hanging out the washing, she became friendly with the sour-faced maid next door, one Betty, who kept house for two old maids called Bennett. Mother talked to her at great length about the convent and about Mother Blessed Margaret, her favourite among the nuns, but Betty hinted darkly that there was nothing she did not know about nuns and chaplains and the dark goings on in convents, and Mother realized, to her great astonishment, that Betty was a Protestant as well. Nobody had ever explained to Mother that Protestants could also be poor. I have a strong impression that from this moment Mother was bent on converting Betty. Betty told Mother that Mr. Bowen was a drunkard, and Mother denied this indignantly, and explained that it was just bad health.

Mother, with her belief in the world of appearances, was always being impressed by the curious mistakes that people made. The Mistress of Studies had been mistaken about the Bowens' house, Betty thought that Mr. Bowen was a drunkard, and Mr. Bowen himself made mistakes that were nearly as bad. One evening his wife, who usually opened the front door when he knocked, was upstairs; Mother opened it instead, and Mr. Bowen beamed on her, put his arm about her waist, and kissed her. She was taken by such a fit of giggling that she was ashamed. "Oh, sir, I'm only

Minnie," she explained, and then went off to the kitchen to laugh in peace at the notion that anybody could take *her* for Mrs. Bowen. She was longing to tell the joke to the mistress, but finally decided that it might seem forward.

But his mistake was nothing to that of Mr. Daly, one of the lodgers, who was a reporter on the Cork *Examiner*. He had a blue overcoat with a velvet collar that Mother thought the height of elegance and which she stroked every time she passed it hanging in the hall. One night she woke and felt a hand on her throat. Her first impulse was to reach for the statue of the Blessed Virgin, which was on the mantelpiece over her bed, but what she grabbed instead was the velvet collar she knew so well.

"Oh, Mr. Daly, is that you?" she cried in relief.

"Don't shout, Minnie!" he whispered crossly. "I'm only looking for the candle."

"But what are you doing in here?" she asked. "Your room is the other way."

"I lost my way in the darkness, that's all," he said with a sigh, and after a couple of minutes went out quietly.

It was only then that Mother, having got over the shock, could laugh in comfort. Here was an educated man with a big job on the Cork *Examiner* who could not even find his own way upstairs in the dark! And she knew from the way he had sighed that this was something that must often happen to him and cause him a great deal of concern.

Next morning, she simply could not resist reporting his mistake to the younger Mrs. Bowen, and then she wished she hadn't, because Mrs. Bowen did not laugh at all. Instead, she rushed upstairs to her husband, who was still in bed, and repeated the story to

him. He jumped out of bed in his nightshirt and went and threw open the door of Daly's room. Mrs. Bowen was still angry when she came downstairs.

"His bed hasn't even been slept in," she said bitterly. "I don't think you need worry, Minnie. I fancy he won't trouble us again."

She was right about that, because in the afternoon a messenger came from the *Examiner* for Daly's clothes, and Mrs. Bowen was still so furious that she hurled them at him from the head of the stairs. She even refused to let Mother parcel them for him. Mother was full of pity for the poor little messenger, who sat at the front gate trying to fold the shirts and suits, but, indeed, I think she was sorrier for poor Mr. Daly, who had been so ashamed of his own mistake that he had walked blindly out of the house and probably got no sleep at all that night. She thought it was very unforeseen of him not to explain to her how seriously Protestants regarded mistakes.

Then the Bowens had a baby, and Mother had one of her many traumatic experiences about him. She made the midwife promise that when she bought the baby, before giving it over to the mother, she would let her see it first, and when Mr. Bowen invited her up to the bedroom to see the new arrival, Mother, after a stunned silence, turned on the midwife and called her a false and wicked woman. Mother hardly ever lost her temper, and never except under what she regarded as intolerable provocation, but when she did, she was magnificent. She reduced everybody to silence. The midwife apologized and excused herself on the ground of the baby's having no clothes, but Mother regarded this as a very lame excuse.

Mother, of course, was enchanted with the baby, and insisted on showing him off to Betty next door.

She had no idea of the emotions she was rousing both in Betty and the two old maids she worked for. One Sunday morning the Bowens stormed back from church and denounced Mother for having said of herself and the baby that she was "bringing up a heretic for Hell." Mother found it difficult to deny this accusation, because she didn't know what a heretic was, even when the Bowens explained that it was something Catholics called Protestants. Mother, weeping, explained that she had never heard Protestants called that by anyone she knew, and finally the Bowens apologized, realizing that they had been victims of a plot of the Bennetts and Betty, but Mother did not lightly recover from the scene. It was quite plain now that Betty would never be a Catholic.

Mother went a few times to the convent to visit my Aunt Margaret, who was seriously ill, her two arms swathed in cotton wool. One day she was sent for, and when she arrived my aunt was dead. The nun who brought her in to see the body told her she should not cry. Margaret was better off. The nun may have been right. It was bad enough to be an orphan, but to be a cripple as well! Margaret's confession had to be heard after that of all the other children because the chaplain had to leave the confession box and sit beside her in her wheel chair. A little while before she died, one of the girls had pushed her wheel chair into the chapel in the evening, and then forgot all about her. The chaplain, too, forgot, and it was only at bedtime that they discovered her missing and found her at last, having sobbed herself to sleep in the deserted chapel.

But the Mistress of Studies, who always seemed to have Mother's best interests at heart, did not forget *her,* and, deciding that it was bad for her to be in a Protestant home, found her a place in a respectable

Catholic lodging house on Richmond Hill. It was kept by a Mrs. Joyce, who had five daughters. The eldest, Kathleen, was Mother's age, and a good-natured girl, but foolish and affected. She spent her life reading sentimental novelettes. As in the Bowens' there were two lodgers, Mannix and Healy—both medical students of a violently patriotic temperament who sometimes came in covered in blood after some political riot—and when Kathleen waited on them they ridiculed her affected airs, but both were fond of Mother and brought her presents of sweets and fruit. Neither of them realized the damage they were doing her in the eyes of her mistress, a coarse and ignorant woman with a violent temper. Every little gift they brought Mother became a further slight on Mrs. Joyce's fine, educated daughter, and she harried Mother relentlessly, shouting "Gerril, do this!" and "Gerril, do that!" One evening she came into the sitting room and saw Mannix pull Mother's pigtail. This was sufficient to put her in one of her usual furies.

"Aha, Gerril!" she said. "The same thing will happen you as happened Madge Murphy."

"What happened her?" Mother asked with genuine interest.

"She had a baby!"

"Well, that isn't true, anyway," Mother said heatedly. (She never liked people to flout her intelligence.) "How could she have a baby when she isn't even married?"

Joyce, who was eating his supper, looked up at his wife as she was about to reply, and said shortly: "Let the child alone! She's better off as she is."

However, that could not keep Mother off the subject of sex, on which her experience with the Bowens had made her an expert. Mrs. Joyce was having her sixth, and Mother, who was nothing if not conscientious, decided to enlighten Patricia, the youngest but one of the children, about the facts of life and the untrustworthiness of midwives. She explained to Patricia that she had personally known a midwife who had promised to show her the baby as soon as she bought it, and, instead of that, had taken it straight up to the mother, concealed. Patricia, who wasn't much more than a baby herself, listened with growing stupefaction and then said: "But you don't *buy* babies."

"Don't you, indeed?" Mother asked good-naturedly. "And how do you get them?"

"You make them, of course," cried Patricia indignantly, and Mother laughed heartily at this example of childish innocence. Her laughter made the little girl furious, and when they reached home she rushed in to her eldest sister, and, pointing an accusing finger at Mother, yelled: "She says you buy babies!"

"Ah, she only says that because you're so young," Kathleen replied good-humouredly.

"She doesn't!" screamed the infant. "She believes it!"

I never had the heart to ask Mother if she had taken example by the child and really learned the facts of life. The one dirty story she knew suggested that she had, but I was never quite certain that she knew what it meant. My impression is that she accepted the evidence in the spirit in which she accepted the evidence of her birth certificate and marked the case "Not Proven." Once in Geneva I overheard an extraordinary conversation between her and a Swiss manufacturer's wife whose son was leaving for Paris and who was very concerned about the sort of women he might meet there.

"It is such a dangerous place for a young man," said the Swiss woman.

"Oh, the traffic!" exclaimed Mother, delighted to have found a kindred spirit. "It took the sight from my eyes."

"And it isn't only the traffic, is it?" the Swiss woman asked gently. "We send them away healthy and we wish them to come back healthy."

"I said it!" Mother cried passionately. "My boy's digestion is never the same."

A certain simplicity of mind that is characteristic of all noble natures, says some old Greek author whose name I cannot remember.

The real nightmare began only after the Joyces moved to a house on Mulgrave Road, near the North Cathedral. Mother no longer had a bedroom, and slept on a trestle bed in the corridor. The painters were still at work in the house, and one of them, after trying in vain to get Mother to walk out with him, proposed to her. He told her he thought she'd make "a damn nice little wife." Mother didn't mind the proposal so much, but she thought his language was terrible.

"What was that fellow saying to you?" Mrs. Joyce asked suspiciously when the painter left the room.

"Ah, nothing, only asking me to marry him," Mother replied lightly, not realizing what she was doing to a woman with five daughters and a probable sixth on the way.

"A queer one he'd be marrying!" growled Mrs. Joyce.

A few days later some nuns of a city order called and addressed Mother, under the impression that she was the eldest of the family, which seemed such a good joke to Patricia that she told her mother. It drove Mrs. Joyce into a tempest of fury.

"A nice daughter, indeed!" snarled Mrs. Joyce. "A creature that doesn't know who she is or where she

61

came from. She doesn't even know who her own mother was."

This was too much for Mother. Insults directed against herself she could stand, but not insults to her mother's memory.

"My mother was a lady, anyhow," she said. "You're not a lady."

After that, Mrs. Joyce made her life a hell. The clothes her previous employer had made fell into rags, and Mrs. Joyce refused to replace them. Instead, she gave Mother a ragged coatee, which she had bought from a dealing woman for a few pence, and an old skirt of her sister's who had just died in the Incurable Hospital. After each meal served to the lodgers, Mrs. Joyce rushed in to gather up the scraps, so that there was nothing left to eat. Hunger was no new thing to any of the orphanage children, but starvation was a new thing to Mother. Instead of candies and biscuits, the medical students now gave her an occasional sixpence, and she bought a loaf of bread, which she concealed, and from which she cut a slice when Mrs. Joyce went out. At night she was so tired that sometimes she never reached her trestle bed in the corridor. Once, walking across the yard with the lamp, she fell asleep and was wakened only by the crash of the falling lamp. Another time, she fell asleep crossing the Joyces' bedroom with a lighted candle, and when she woke up the curtains were in flames about her.

Then her long beautiful hair grew lousy, and Mrs. Joyce ordered her to cut it off. Mother did not perceive that this was the chance the woman had been waiting for all the time. Slight her beautiful, educated daughter indeed! She would show the medical students what a girl looked like when she was ragged and starved and without hair.

That evening, when Mother served the dinner, Mannix looked at her in astonishment. "What the hell did you do that to yourself for?" he shouted, and when she had told him he went on: "For God's sake, girl, will you get out of this house before that woman does something worse to you? Can't you see yourself that she hates you?"

"But why would she hate me?" asked Mother.

"Because she's jealous of you. That's why."

But Mother could not see why anyone should be jealous of somebody as poor and friendless as herself. I doubt if it occurred to her to the day of her death that the Mistress of Studies was also jealous of her. With that simplicity of mind the old author praised, she never really understood the hatred that common natures entertain for refined ones.

She was now ashamed to leave the house, even to buy food. And then something happened that showed how far she had really sunk. The Good Shepherd nuns had at last learned that the lodgers in the house were medical students, and medical students were notorious for their depravity, though this instantly ceased the moment they got a degree. It is a superstition from the early days of scientific medicine, and it has not yet died out. One day two nuns came to the house in a covered car, and ordered Mother to return to the orphanage with them. She refused, and they reminded her of the penalty she was incurring. Any girl who left one of the pleasant homes provided by the nuns without permission was not allowed to return to the orphanage, which was the only home most of the girls had. In the same way, one who refused to leave immediately when ordered was not allowed to return. Mother still refused to go back with them, and when they left in anger, she knew she had now no place in the world to go. When

63

I tried to get her to explain this extraordinary conduct, she said, almost impatiently, that she could not go back in that state among clean, well-dressed girls. Possibly behind her refusal to return there was an element of almost hysterical vanity, but that cannot be the real explanation. My own guess is that it was despair, rather than vanity. Children, and adolescents who have retained their childish innocence have little hold on life. They have no method of defending themselves against the things that are not in their own nature. I think that, without knowing it, Mother hated the nuns for what they had made of her innocent life, and had already decided to commit suicide. Her parents were dead, Margaret had died while she was at Bowens', Tim she had seen only once for a few hours in all the years, and she had nothing left to live for.

For eight or nine months longer, it dragged on like that. The eldest girl took pity on her, helped with the housework when her mother wasn't looking, and even checked her mother when her scurrility went too far. The youngest also helped in her own enlightened way, hiding Mother's brushes and mops and dusters in order to be able to ask: "Minnie, what are you looking for? I get it for you." Even in her own misery, Mother laughed at the baby's good-will. But one winter day Joyce came in at one o'clock for his dinner and it wasn't ready. His wife ordered Mother out of the house. She put off the apron she had been wearing, put on her black straw hat, threw the ragged old coatee over her shoulders— the hat, jacket and skirt were all the possessions she had left in the world—and went out onto Mulgrave Road. She saw people stop and stare at her, and realized the extraordinary figure she cut. She ran up a laneway by the North Infirmary and threw the ragged jacket there, but people still continued to look. She ran

64

for shelter to the Dominican Church on the Sand Quay, and prayed.

She knew now that only one hope remained to her, and that a miracle. None of the nuns—not even her favourite, Mother Blessed Margaret—could overrule the Mistress of Studies, and if she went to the orphanage she would be turned away. She knew too many to whom it had happened. The only one who could overrule the Mistress of Studies was Reverend Mother. It was she who had arranged for my grandmother's funeral. But lay sisters, not Reverend Mothers, answer convent door bells, and from one o'clock until darkness fell Mother waited in the church, most of the time on her knees, praying for a miracle to happen. She had decided that if it didn't she would return to the river and drown herself. It was only when she was telling me about this period of her life that I ever heard her use such an expression in any matter that concerned herself, for not only did she believe suicide was wrong, she thought it demonstrative, and she was almost fiercely undemonstrative in grief or pain. Nor, when she talked of that afternoon, as an old woman, did she exaggerate it. Father and I, with our deep streak of melancholia, would have added something to it that, by making it more dramatic, would also have made it less terrible. It is an awful moment when gaiety dies in those who have no other hold on life.

On the dark, stepped pathway up to the convent, she met two ladies who were coming away from it, chattering, and paid no heed to them. She went up the steps to the front door and rang, and immediately the door opened and Reverend Mother stood inside. In sheer relief, Mother broke down and began to sob out her story. Reverend Mother did not recognize her at first; then something seemed to strike her. "Aren't you

the girl we told to come back from that terrible house?"
she asked.

"Yes," said Mother.

"And why *didn't* you come?"

"I had no clothes. I was ashamed."

"It's strange I should have answered the door,"
said Reverend Mother. "I was just seeing off some
friends, and something kept me here thinking. I was
just walking up and down the corridor." Clearly, she
was aware of the coincidence, but Mother knew it was
something more.

She brought Mother into her own parlour, sat
her before the fire to warm herself, and rang the bell
for the Mistress of Studies.

"Minnie O'Connor has come back from that terrible house to stay," she said quietly, and then as the Mistress of Studies burst into a stream of abuse she added:
"Don't scold, Mother!"

Turning to Mother, the Mistress of Studies cried:
"If you're in that state, you can go to the workhouse.
You will not stay here!"

"She is not in that state, and she will stay here,"
Reverend Mother said firmly, and that night, for the
first time in years, Mother had enough to eat, and
bathed, and slept in a clean bed.

She never made much of her own misery. Other
girls, as she said, had had a worse time. But she never
ceased to speak of what happened as a miracle, and,
in the way of those to whom miracles occur, never by
so much as a harsh word attempted to blame the Mistress of Studies. Not that she did not realize that for
the future she must be on her guard. I feel sure it was
significant that when, a week later, the Mistress of
Studies found her another nice home, in a public house
off Blarney Lane that was a lodging house for cattle

dealers, Mother, without even unpacking her bag, returned to the convent and told the Mistress of Studies that it was not a suitable place for a young woman. It was also significant that, a few days later, the Mistress of Studies was replaced by Mother's great friend, Mother Blessed Margaret, whom I knew and loved when she was an old lady. Old or young, she, like Reverend Mother, was a lady.

4

MOTHER BLESSED MARGARET'S way with the
girls was to say: "There is a situation free
in the X's. I think you might try it and see what you
think of it." So Mother took a situation with the Stew-
arts, and after sticking it for six months did not think
much of it. Mr. Stewart came from the North of Ireland, and was a tight-fisted, small, dark, dingy man.
Every morning he ground and prepared his own coffee
on the landing. His wife was very tall, thin, ailing, de-
vout, and fussy. There were two daughters. Kathleen,
the eldest, took after her father; Nan was small, with
frizzy fair hair and a good-natured friendly manner,
and was forever singing Methodist hymns. Mrs. Stewart, as Mother described her, had a lot in common with
Trollope's Mrs. Proudie. Once when a girl called Ethel

Richards was staying with them, Kathleen and Nan chaffed her about her young man.

"Do tell us what his name is!" one of the girls cried.

"Oh!" Ethel said ecstatically. "That name above all other names!"

At this, Mrs. Stewart sat up in her chair, red with horror and indignation.

"Ethel!" she cried. "Unsay those words!"

Mrs. Proudie could scarcely have phrased it better. But for Mother it was too like the dingy atmosphere of the Bowens' house. Then Mother Blessed Margaret got her the job that for eight years was to provide her with a real home, and for the rest of her days with memories that I can only describe as enchanted. It was in a house whose gardens reached to the convent wall, so that Mother could talk to the nuns across it, and it was occupied by a butter-and-egg merchant named Barry and his unmarried sister, Alice. I do not think life can ever have been as good anywhere as it seemed to Mother there, but for the orphan girl who had never asked anything but that people should value her, it was happiness enough. Ned Barry was a man of forty, tall and fat, with a hook nose and high colour. His main weakness was vanity, but he was the kindest of men and the gayest, and she loved gaiety even more than she loved kindness. When she told me about him, later in life, I did not guess what now seems so obvious—that she was very much in love with him—nor did I wonder, as I now find myself doing, whether he was not just a little attracted by her. She admitted that he had been "flighty" with her, and she was not the sort of woman who admitted, or permitted, "flightiness."

He gave great stag parties, and after them the men had to be carried up to bed, and Mother brought them their breakfast of whisky and soda in the morning, while their wives sat in the hall waiting for them to get up. There was a piano in Barry's bedroom, and sometimes the party was resumed there by men in their nightshirts who played the piano and danced hornpipes by the hour. To judge by Mother's accounts, all the men were unbelievably good, brave, and generous, and often there would be as much as twenty-five shillings in tips on the hall table in the morning. Twenty-five shillings was big money for a poor girl who up to the age of eighteen had had no wages at all, and she saved it, though I suspect my Uncle Tim, who was now an apprentice in a cobbler's shop in Barrack Street, lightened it considerably.

One day he called to the house to ask for money and to say good-bye. That night he stowed away on a cattle boat, was discovered and brought before the captain, and then put ashore in an English port. He tramped across England to Colchester, where he enlisted, and Mother did not see him again for some years till Alice came to her in great distress and said: "Minnie, there are two soldiers here, asking for you, and I'm afraid they'll run away with Towser." But when Alice discovered that one of them was Mother's brother, she set to making supper with her and produced a bottle of her brother's whisky.

She was like that, a magnificent woman with a great head of golden hair, and she had all her brother's good nature. From the beginning the two girls were never mistress and maid. Alice had had a succession of servants who were drunkards or thieves, and was glad of Mother, and Mother had had a succession of heartless mistresses, and was grateful for one who treated her as a friend. Alice confided her love affairs to Mother, and I have no doubt that if Mother had love affairs, she confided them to Alice. Alice had few friends,

and she and Mother spent the summer afternoons taking long walks or sitting under a hedge by the river
while Alice painted a water colour and Mother read a
book. When the two went to town together, people
stopped in the street to stare at Alice's beauty, and
Mother was as proud as though it were at her own. But
Alice had periods of depression that sometimes lasted
for a whole week, and all that time she did not speak,
and after the first few months Mother, believing that
Alice was going insane, gave notice. Alice apologized,
and Mother became even more devoted to her than she
already was to her brother. I can answer for their mu-
tual affection, because by a curious coincidence I was
able to bring them together again when they were elderly women, and they rattled on delightedly like two
schoolgirls who had not met for a whole vacation.

Each of them had had one son: Alice's had died
tragically under a cloud, the sort of cloud that Irish re-
spectability creates over a mere indiscretion; I was just
beginning to make a small reputation for myself; and
even the touch of envy on Alice's part, of complacency
on Mother's, could not conceal the deep affection between two women who had shared real happiness together.

It was the great age of the butter-and-egg trade.
The Barrys were wealthy and lived in a beautiful house,
with gardens before and behind producing strawber-
ries, raspberries, pears, apples, and peaches. Like the
Jewish merchants of the time, the Catholic merchants
did things in style, far beyond the level of their Protestant neighbours. Like the Jews, they were emerging
from an age of persecution, and, full of self-confidence,
were the principal supporters of Charles Stewart Parnell. His fall was the first real shock to their self-confidence. On the day he died, Alice came down to the

kitchen to tell Mother, and the two of them sat there all evening, weeping.

Meanwhile, the great stag parties went on, catered for by a restaurant in town, and the big house was always full of life, for Barry was so good-natured that he could not pass a policeman on his beat without bringing him home for a drink, or a poor prostitute without bringing her home for a meal, and often when Mother came down to the kitchen in the morning the pantry was bare and the decanter empty. Half the girls in town seemed to want to marry him, but his sister took their letters from the hall stand and, having read them out scornfully to Mother, destroyed them. Of course, he never noticed. He was a rattlepate and never in time for anything. He would arrange to take Alice to the theatre, and she would dress and wait for him, but he never showed up on time. After the performance had already begun, he would rush in in a frenzy of efficiency and dash upstairs to dress, with Mother at his heels to fix the studs in his dress shirt. But Alice was endlessly patient with him.

Then a child, a niece who had been left an orphan, came to live with them, and soon after that Alice married. She married because she felt she ought to be married rather than because she really wanted to marry. I suspect she was one of those dreamy, romantic women whose marriage, to be successful, must first make smithereens of their personality, but, in the way of women like that, she drew back from the danger. She had been very much in love with a doctor, but refused to marry him because he drank. He took up with another girl, and one day when the three of them met at the races, he threw his arms about Alice and said: "I have you now, and I'll never let you go." "Oh, yes, you will," the other girl said, not in the least discomposed, and detached him from Alice. Alice came home in a state of collapse. The kind, bookish man she finally married was not the sort to make smithereens of anyone, and she returned from the honeymoon in despair. "I should never have left Ned," she told Mother. When it was all over and Alice was settled with her husband in a little village in East Cork, Mother was sick with loneliness. While the child stayed with them, Barry pulled himself together and took Mother and her to the Opera House every week, but when she went off to school, he did his entertaining in a hotel in the city, and Mother lay awake half the night listening for the sound of his step. The old house was full of noises and had the reputation of being haunted.

Reverend Mother insisted that she must not stay on in the house unchaperoned, and pressed her to leave, but Mother hated to do that. Her reputation never worried her much at any time. There were good people and bad people, and she had her own standards of both, and the reputation she might retain by not associating with people she thought good did not interest her. She had been happier there than she had ever been in her life before, and she clung to her position like an old dog to a deserted house, waiting for Alice's brief visits and the child's return from school. When she had been living there for a year without a chaperon, Reverend Mother issued an ultimatum: Mother must choose between Barry and her, between the house and the convent. Mother wrote distractedly to Alice, who replied shrewdly that Mother should take in another of the orphans as maid. Reverend Mother refused to accept the suggestion, saying that Barry's reputation was too bad. This is the point in the story at which I begin to wonder whether Reverend Mother's ultimatum was not directed at him rather than at her—she may well have been trying to prevent Mother's staying on as housekeeper so that she could come back as mistress of the house. I am quite sure that Mother never considered that aspect of it at all. She was blinded to everything in the world by the fact that she regarded the house as her home.

Terrified of a breach with Reverend Mother, Mother at last gave notice and told Barry that the nuns refused to let her remain. He was bitterly offended.

"The nuns are no friends of yours, Minnie," he said —a phrase that, again, could mean something different from what she saw in it. I have a suspicion, which may be mere day-dreaming, that he had considered marrying her, and that only his vanity had kept him back. The man who married his housekeeper was too obvious a subject for ridicule. And now that she had given notice, Mother was almost insane with worry and fear and loneliness. Finally, unable to bear it any longer, she told her friends in the convent that she intended to remain on, and withdrew her notice. But now it was *his* turn to be stiff. He told her that he had already engaged another housekeeper, and, seeing her gesture of love slighted, she grew really angry. She told him curtly that it was just as well that way. It wasn't, as she soon discovered. When she tried to show the new housekeeper, a crude country girl, the workings of the house, she showed no interest, and spent her time in Mother's bedroom, trying on her hats.

The night the covered car came to take Mother and her trunk away, she was broken-hearted. All she had ever asked was a home, and for eight years she had had a perfect one, with a man and woman she loved and who valued her love, and she knew that no other house in the world would mean as much to her. It was, as she said, the tragedy of the orphan, who clings to any place where she is happy. She still went back in the mornings, to try and train the new housekeeper, and afterwards, during the school holidays, to act as companion to Barry's niece and buy whatever she needed. The new housekeeper, who by this time had managed to introduce her mother into the house to help her, and later brought her sisters in as well, was very cordial and insisted on showing all the presents she received from Barry. One day as Mother and she were passing through his bedroom, she pointed slyly to a pair of women's slippers under his bed. "He gave me them too," she said.

Mother did not see Barry again until six years later, when she was married and I a baby in her arms. During the first three of these she was employed in four houses, sufficient indication of the fever of restlessness in which she found herself. After Barrys' she found it impossible to settle anywhere, and that, too, I think, is part of the orphan pattern. For me, it was best illustrated in one of the most moving stories she told about the orphanage. Reverend Mother, whose brother, a priest, had died young, was convinced that the reason for his death was that he, like other priests, was confined to the dragons who in Ireland become priests' housekeepers. She decided to train as housekeepers a few of the orphans who had real intelligence, and one of these, May Corcoran, first underwent training in a really good town house and was then sent as housekeeper to a young priest in the country. After six months she returned to the orphanage, nobody knew why. She went out again as housekeeper to a priest of more settled age and again in a short time she returned. This time the secret was out. She had "made herself cheap"—that is, she had fallen in love with each priest in turn, until her innocent adoration of him and concern for his comfort had made him a laughing-stock among his fellow priests and his parishioners. The experiment of training priests' housekeepers was at an end, and May was found a job as nursery governess with a wealthy family who were delighted with her gentleness and gracious manners. She, on the other hand, filled with restlessness and resentment, had no affection to spare for them. She fell ill and an operation became necessary, but she refused to undergo it in Cork. She arranged for her admission to a Dublin hospital and on the evening before the operation was to take place, destroyed every particle of writing by which she could be identified, and then went into the hospital and died after the operation. Only a letter from Reverend Mother that had slipped down inside the lining of her coat showed who she was.

Mother's restlessness led her to take a job in England, but she stood this only six months, and preferred to repay the advance that she had received for her passage money. By August of '98 she was in a position in East Cork with a well-to-do family of millers who behaved in the way of lords of the manor in England, had their old pensioners to the house every Saturday to draw their pensions, and gave expensive entertainments to the children of their mill-hands at Christmas. The lady of the house was the daughter of a general much in favour with the Queen, who was godmother to the second son—called, of course, Victor—and presented him with a silver baby service. The second maid was a girl from Limerick called Molly, who arrived while Victor was being born, with references that were not checked until later and that turned out to have been forged. Molly was the mistress of a son in another big house closer to Cork, and had taken the situation to be nearer him. When he wished to take her off on holiday,

Molly sent herself a wire announcing that her father was dying, and went off, wearing Mrs. Armitage's jewellery and clothes. Molly returned from the holiday and presented herself before Mrs. Armitage wearing a gold locket that had been one of Mrs. Armitage's wedding presents. When she looked at it and took it, Molly tried to grab it back. Discharged next morning, she wrote from Cork to say that she was employing a solicitor, but, she added, "what better could you expect from a woman who did not go to Confession and Communion?" Like many of her race, Molly believed firmly in the superiority of faith over morals.

Here at least Mother was able to visit Alice Barry and her husband. By this time Tim had become engaged, and Alice insisted on Mother's bringing him and his girl as well. There was a brief interlude when one of the orphans induced her to take a job outside Limerick where the boss and the Swiss butler, Armady, fought a running battle in the manner of *Figaro* as to which was to pay attention to the maids. In 1901 she took a job with the family of a naval paymaster in Queenstown. In the meantime Tim had married; his daughter, Julia, was born on a Saturday and on the following Monday he set sail from Queenstown for the South African War. He had to be carried, blind drunk, on to the troopship while Mother held his hand, and my conscientious father, afraid he would die of thirst on the long voyage, hurled bottle after bottle of whisky on board, to be caught by his comrades. As the troopship moved away, my uncle distinguished himself further by trying to throw himself overboard, but his companions caught and held him. Along with a holy medal, Mother had given him her gunmetal watch, which contained a photograph of Mother Blessed Margaret. On the second day out, he staked it at cards and lost it. That was typical of Tim. But it was also typical of him to order from London an expensive gold watch to replace it, and in his letters he continued to warn her against my father. "Have nothing to do with Mick Donovan," he wrote. "He's a good friend, but he'll make a poor husband." Poor man, I'm afraid he did.

The marriage may have been precipitated by a mean trick of the paymaster's wife. She brought Mother on a long holiday to her own mother's house in Sheerness as nurse to her daughter, aged five, but in England she decided that what she really wanted was an English nurse, and she proposed to bring her back to Ireland on the return half of Mother's ticket. Without consulting Mother, she arranged employment for her as parlourmaid in a house in the dockyards. "I told you I would not live in this country," Mother said angrily. "I came with you and I intend to go back with you." On her return she married Father, and they went to live with his parents, who then had a house in Maryville Cottages in Barrackton that they could not afford to keep on their own. There was some ugly story about this incident, but I have forgotten the details. I know that Mother was disgusted and horrified by the dirt and drunkenness and complained that it had not been part of their bargain. I think it was probably Father who said: "It's done now, and it can't be undone," because the words rankled in her mind for forty years. When he went off to the South African War, she took rooms with Miss Wall in Douglas Street, and I was born when he was still away. When he returned they set up house in Blarney Lane, and Mother opened a little shop. This was the one period of her life that she always refused to speak about, and it was clearly a horror to her. The whole idea of her keeping a shop was absurd, because she could never refuse anybody anything, and when at

78

last she had to abandon it she was owed money all over the place. But I don't think Father gave her any chance of continuing. For Tim had proved to be a prophet. Father drank his way through the shop, and with it all her other treasures, including Tim's gold watch, which she sold for five pounds.

One morning at Mass in Sunday's Well Church, I cried and had to be taken out onto the porch. The church door opened and Ned Barry came out. Mother was horrified at his appearance. He was pale and hollow-cheeked, and she felt sure he was dying. In the old, good-natured way he stopped to speak to me and pat me on the head, as he would have done with any baby, but without once looking at her or recognizing her, and she was too taken aback to remind him of who she was. He had reached the chapel gate before she made a move. But he was a brisk walker, and she was burdened with me, and, hard as she ran, she could only keep him in view down the length of Sunday's Well, till he turned in the gateway of his house. As the door closed behind him, she ran up the avenue. She rang the bell, and the housekeeper put her head out of a bedroom window.

"The Boss isn't in," she said shortly.

"I saw him go in just a moment ago," said Mother.

"Well, he's not in now, anyway," the other woman said, and banged the window shut.

When Mother saw Barry again a few months later, he was dead. Alice had looked through the house, which was filthy, and found a compromising letter from the housekeeper to a man, inviting him to the house while her mother was at the church. The lawyers, too, had stepped in and cancelled the order for a piano which the housekeeper had issued for her own entertainment. Alice and she sat with the body in the bedroom of the house where all three of them had been so happy together. I was put to sleep on the sofa beside him, and the two women talked till night fell of his kindness and his charm, while the housekeeper and her many relations sat below in the kitchen and did not once approach them.

5

I SUSPECT THAT it was that house, rather than the convent, that really left its mark upon my mother's character and established, if it did not give her, standards of behaviour that would have been exacting in any social group and were impossible in the gutter where the world had thrown her. She rarely permitted herself to comment on any tiny treachery she had observed in one of my friends, and I used to persuade myself that she had not noticed, but if worse happened, and she felt free to speak, it became clear that she had seen every detail and felt it more than I. Sometimes she observed things that nobody else had observed. Once I laughed outright at her when she said of a brilliant young artist who came to the flat: "I'd have

nothing to do with that boy. There's a streak of imbe-
cility in him," but time proved her right.

She rarely asked anything for herself, never made
scenes, and often went for months without the com-
monest necessities rather than complain. On her seven-
tieth birthday she had a very bad fall, and the doctor
who examined her told me that all her life she had suffered from chronic appendicitis. When she really did
want something—usually something that involved the
pleasure of a third party, like the cousins of mine to
whom in her last years she was devoted—she dripped
hints like a leaky old tap. On the other hand, "hints" is a
crude word for the photograph casually dropped where
I would be bound to see it, or for the gossamer off-key
phrases that seemed to be intended as a sort of psycho-
logical conditioning that might ultimately influence my
conduct subconsciously; and I noticed that when the
hints went on too long and I shouted at her, she seemed
to be less hurt by the shout than by my discovery of her
innocent little plot. At such moments, I fancy, she
probably blamed herself severely for a lack of delicacy.

That curious negative energy gave her an almost
uncanny power of inducing people to confide in her.
She woke very early, with a passion for tea, and when
we were staying in a London hotel I made a deal with
the chambermaid to bring it to her when she herself came on duty. When I called for her at nine o'clock
Mother had acquired the material for a full-length
novel of life in Devon from the maid. On the same
morning I had an interview with my agent, and left
her sitting in Trafalgar Square. When I returned forty-
five minutes later, a good-looking woman was sitting beside her. Mother had got the material for another novel.
By that time she knew as much about the life of ordinary people in England as I would learn in years. She

was uncomfortable abroad even more than I was but for the same reason—all that lovely material going to waste—but in Switzerland she met the Swiss woman who spoke English and got her life story as well.

Naturally, with that sort of mind she loved novels, particularly Victorian novels, but she had a similar passion for classical music. She made a point of never intruding on me, because I might be "thinking," but she reserved her rights in respect of thinking to music, and I had only to put the needle on a phonograph record to see her shuffle in, smiling, her shawl round her shoulders, and settle on the chair nearest the door. The smile, as well as the choice of chair, clearly indicated that she was not disturbing me because she wasn't really there. Sometimes if I had visitors she didn't want to interrupt, she would give the handle of my door a gentle twist, leave the door ajar, and then sit on a chair outside. She had a passion for Schubert and Mozart, and loved soprano voices and violins—the high, pure, piercing tone. It took me longer to discover her taste in fiction, because her comments on anything were so direct and simple that they could appear irrelevant. She talked as a child talks, completely without self-consciousness. Once she practically burst into tears when I brought her a novel of Walter Scott's and cried: "But you know I can't read Scotch!" It took me years to discover that she didn't really like dialect. Another time I brought her a novel by Peadar O'Donnell, whom she loved, but she had read only a few pages when I saw her getting fretful.

"What is it now?" I growled.

"Ah, didn't you notice?" she asked reproachfully, looking at me over her glasses. "Nearly every sentence begins with 'I.' "

From remarks like these one had to deduce what

83

she meant, but often no deductions were necessary.
Once I took her on a funicular to the top of some Alp,
and as we sat on the terrace of a restaurant far above
the glittering lake, I enthused about the view. "There
should be great drying up here," she said thoughtfully,
her mind reverting to the problem of laundry.

In spite of her gentleness, there was a streak of
terribleness in her—something that was like a Last
Judgement, and (as I suspect the Last Judgement will
be) rather less than just. I think it was linked in a curious way with her weakness for tearing up pictures of
herself that she didn't like and removing pictures of
the woman she disapproved of from photograph albums, and echoed some childish magic, some recon-
struction of reality to make it less intolerable. During
court proceedings about my right to visit my children,
after my wife and I were separated, Mother learned
that they were in court and, against my wishes, insisted on seeing them. I went with her to the witnesses'
room, and when the children saw her they slunk away
with their heads down. She went up to them slowly,
her two hands out, as she had gone up to the mad boy
in Blarney Lane, saying in a whisper: "Darlings, won't
you speak to me? It's only Dunnie." (Dunnie was their
pet name for her.) I could bear it no longer, and, putting my arm round her, made her leave the room. She
stood against the wall outside with her face suddenly
gone white and stony, and said: "I'm eighty-five, but
I've learned a new thing today. I've learned that you can
turn children into devils." Then and later I argued angrily with her, pleading that you cannot hold children
responsible for what they do when they are frightened,
but she never spoke their names again. I insisted on
speaking to her about them, and she listened politely
because she knew I was doing what I thought "right,"

which was the only test of conduct she admitted, but she offered no opinion, and it was clear that their photographs had been taken out of whatever album she carried in her mind. The woman who all her life had sought love could not entertain the idea of a child who, she thought, rejected it.

A couple of weeks before that, our next-door neighbour in the little "development" where we lived had died. His younger daughter had put in a good deal of unpaid work as secretary of the Tenants' Association. But the family was Protestant, and by this time Irish Catholics no longer attended Protestant funerals—a refinement of conscience that had completely escaped Mother's attention. She only realized it when the funeral was ready to start and none of the hundred families in the estate development had shown up. I was waiting at the front door, with my coat and hat on, and as she rushed out I tried to detain her. "How dare you!" she cried frantically. "Let me go! Do you think I could let that poor woman go with her husband's body to the grave thinking that those miserable cowards are Catholics?" She ran out in front of the house, her grey hair blowing in the wind, and held out her hands to the widow. "I'm old and feeble, or I'd be along with you today," she said, glaring round at the estate houses, where people watched from behind drawn blinds. "What those creatures are doing to you—that's not Catholic; that's not Irish."

When she was dead, and I had done all the futile things she would have wished, like bringing her home across the sea to rest with Father, and when the little girl who had refused to speak to her in court had knelt beside the coffin in the luggage van at Kingsbridge, and the little boy had joined the train at Limerick Junction, I returned to the house she had left. When she fell ill, I had been teaching the child who was left me a Negro spiritual, and now when we came home together and I opened the front door, he felt that everything was going to be the same again and that we could go back to our singing. He began, in a clear treble: "Child, I know you're going to miss me when I'm gone." Then only did I realize that the horror that had haunted me from the time I was his age and accompanied Mother to the orphanage, and learned for the first time the meaning of parting and death, had happened at last to me, and that it made no difference to me that I was fifty and a father myself.

And I await the resurrection from the dead and eternal life to come.

MINNIE O'DONOVAN AND THE AUTHOR
AGED FOUR MONTHS

II

I KNOW WHERE I'M GOING

6

THERE WAS ONLY one thing to be said in favour of Father's home ground—it was colourful. There were fifteen houses in the little square, and the occupants were as sharply distinguished as though they had all been of different races and religions. They had little appeal to me, because I dreamed of families that lived in the Ballyhooley Road, who kept their front doors shut, played the piano in the evenings, and did not go to the neighbours' houses to borrow a spoon of tea or a cupful of sugar, but they are all very distinct in my memory.

In one house lodged a married couple who provided a strange counterpoint to my own parents. Mrs. MacCarthy was a big, bosomy woman with a round, rosy face who was the living image of Kathleen Ma-

vourneen in the picture in our kitchen, and must have
been a girl of great beauty. Her personality was like her
looks, warm and sunny, and she had a deep, husky
voice. Her husband was a small, taciturn man who
worked in the Harbour Commissioners. At regular intervals, Mrs. MacCarthy went on batters that were as
bad as those of my father in their utter destructiveness.
Mother would rescue her from the road where she had
fallen, and bring her home, caked with blood and dirt,
and wash her face and comb her hair, while she
scolded her gently. "Ah, Mrs. MacCarthy," she would
say, "indeed and indeed you should be ashamed of
yourself, making an exhibition of yourself like that,
and what will your poor husband say?" But by this
time Mrs. MacCarthy would be threatening what she
would do that miserable little gnat of a man when he
came home.

The woman who lived in the house on our left was
a Cockney called Gertie Twomey. At first, I think, she
lodged with my grandmother, and then took over the
house when Grandmother came to live with us. She had
married a nice gentle Cork sailor called Steve Twomey
who had picked her up on one of his trips and brought
her home in the spirit in which he would have brought
home some flaming, chattering parakeet from the
Congo to hang with his dispirited goldfinches and ca-
naries. She was a tiny little woman with a face shaped
like a box and coloured a brilliant red as though she
never drank anything but gin, though I have no recollection of her drinking at all. In the middle of the box
was a gleaming snub nose like a holy medal, and above
it two small, crafty, merry eyes that seemed as though
they had been sunk into the head with a metal-worker's
tool. She haunted our house, perhaps because Father,
as a travelled man, could talk to her about London, or

perhaps because Mother, as a superior woman and a good housekeeper, might be expected to understand her scorn of the "natives." She usually came accompanied by her two pretty daughters, one attached to either hand and trailing behind in the wind of her approach like afterthoughts—"pore little eyengils," as she called them with a sudden brilliant glare that was probably supposed to suggest mother love—and the beady little eyes started to flicker inquisitively about the kitchen in quest of anything new or useful. She missed nothing, had no shyness about asking for anything she wanted, and distressed Mother, who preferred the shyer manner of the "natives." "A great maker-out," Mother sometimes called her with real disapproval.

Gertie thought Irish Catholics impractical, and small wonder, for behind the English sentimentality and gab was a mind like a razor. I suppose she had had to become a Catholic to marry Steve, but the Catholicism had not taken. As a girl in London, Gertie had heard all about the bloke in the Holy Land who started religion, and knew that his idea was to give things away to people who wanted them, a view that was the very opposite of that held by the Catholic priests in Ireland. They acted as though the bloke in the Holy Land had intended them to get the dibs, but they couldn't take Gertie in with that sort of nonsense. I doubt if any priest looking for dues ever got a penny out of her. He didn't have two kids to keep, as she did, and if money ever changed hands—which I doubt—it must have been in the other direction. "Why," she said one day, grabbing a gold chain on the priest's fat belly, "that beautiful gold chain you're wearing would keep me and my two poor helpless little angels for months. . . . And wasn't I right?" she added sharply, reporting the incident to Father and Mother, who didn't know where

to look. Mother out of a sense of duty would have given
the priest her last half-crown, as I suspect she often did,
and Father, whose views of religion were always a mystery to me, would have been afraid to refuse him.
Though always very respectful to priests, he didn't like
them and thought them unlucky, like magpies, and
though he went to Mass regularly, he never attended
the Sacraments. He probably thought them unlucky
too. At the same time, with English practicality Gertie
also had English tolerance and grit. Not only did she not
hold it against the priest that he hadn't given her his
gold watch and chain; she rather enjoyed the tussle
for it.

However, her great entries were reserved for
stormy nights when Father was sitting under the lamp,
reading the *Echo*. Steve worked on an old tub called the
Hannibal that must have been about the one age with
Carthage, and when a big wind began blowing up the
river, Gertie, with her vivid imagination, immediately
began to picture it at the bottom of the Irish Sea, herself
a widow, and her two little angels orphans. On nights
like these she could not remain at home. She had to
know what Father, the universal expert, made out of
the shipping news. We would hear her bang the front
door of her house, chattering like a monkey to herself
or the children, and then came the hasty shuffle of her
feet down the channel in front of our house as she
dragged the children behind her to our squeaking gate.
"It's that woman again!" Mother would say in disgust,
and the string of the latch would be pulled, and Gertie
would be framed in the kitchen doorway, her hair wild,
her shiny face, which seemed to be haunted, reflecting
the lamplight. Her right hand would be raised in a dramatic gesture.

"'Ark to that!" she would mutter as the wind

howled in the yard outside. "The sea must be mountains high. Nothing could ever live through that."

"Oh, now, now, Mrs. Twomey! I wouldn't let myself be upset by a bit of wind like that," Father would say gravely, in the ingenuous belief that he was really comforting her instead of driving her mad. Father was an intensely conventional man, and he knew that this was how a woman whose husband was at sea on a stormy night should feel, and that this was the sort of thing you should say to her.

"A bit of wind?" she would mutter wonderingly. "How can you, Mr. O'Donovan! You know that ship should have been scrapped years ago. I warned him! Now he has only himself to blame."

"Ah, well," Father would say, doing the hob-lawyer, which seemed to be what was expected of him, "a lot would depend on what it was like at sea, or what way the ship was going."

"It's in the hands of God," Mother would say. "You should be praying for him."

Now, this was the sort of talk that Gertie didn't like at all. Praying was what the natives did when there was nothing to eat in the house, instead of going after the sky pilots with horse, foot, and artillery.

"God helps those who help themselves," she snapped. "I told him years ago to get off that boat. I have my children to think of, don't I? This time tomorrow they may be orphans." Her eyes settled unseeingly on the children, and she asked menacingly: "What'll you do when you have no father?" At this they would burst into loud harmonious wails that for some reason seemed to give her deep satisfaction, because she beamed and patted them and assured them fondly that Mummy would look after them.

I never saw a woman who got so much value out

of her troubles, but they were too intense to last. Having exhausted all the phases of her tragedy—the terrors of the deep, the temptations of widowhood, and the sad fate of orphaned children—in ten or fifteen minutes, she hadn't much more left to grieve for and began to see the bright side of things. Or rather, she became practical, and you saw what was really behind all that English guff. She sat bolt upright in her chair, her little eyes half shut as they darted shrewdly from Father to Mother, to see how they were taking it. Mother was not taking it too well. Having been an orphan herself, she did not like to see it turned into a subject for play-acting. Father was completely mystified. He had a conventional mind, and a slow one, and he never really saw where Gertie was getting.

Compensation was now her theme—purely for the children's sake, of course. She knew several sailors' widows who had been impractical in the usual Irish way. They should have got more compensation, and they should have handled more wisely whatever they had got. The English were better at handling lump sums than the Irish. And, of course, though wages were bad and jobs uncertain, they did bring in the regular dibs while no one could be sure of a lump sum unless it was invested wisely. She would have a solicitor on the job to see that she got her rights, and then she would have enough to buy or rent a big house in London which she would run as a superior boarding house, furnished in style and confined to lodgers of the best class. There her children would get a real education, not the sort of thing that passed for education among the natives. The first thing she would buy would be a piano, and they would have lessons and grow up as real little ladies. There was something about being able to play the piano that raised a girl in a man's estimation, wasn't there?

And subtly, almost imperceptibly, as she talked her tone changed, and she was no longer practical but giddy and gay. That was where Father's reminiscences of London came in handy, because they reassured her that everything was as she remembered it, with parks and bands and music-halls and toffs, and all at once, her red face beaming, she began to run her fingers over the keys of an imaginary piano and sang in a cracked voice:

> *O, won't we have a merry time,*
> *Drinking whisky, beer and wine,*
> *On Coronation Day?*

By this time she would be in the highest of spirits, cracking jokes and making the children laugh. But, as though she found it difficult to sustain any mood for long, that, too, would pass and she would remember her bad neighbours and her many wrongs and snap at the children to tell them keep quiet and not break their mummy's heart. In those days I did not understand it, and I doubt if my parents understood it either, but nowadays I fancy she was thinking that even if the wind was still howling about the house, the old ship had weathered worse, and she would never return to dear old London Town but end her days among ignorant Irish Catholics, who didn't even know what the bloke in the Holy Land had said about giving people things. Then she would accuse the children of having no heart, and when they cried she would spank them till Mother protested, and finally she would shuffle off as she had come, into the storm, dragging the yelling kids behind her and muttering rapidly to herself. No wonder Mother told Minnie Connolly that she was "never right."

95

7

BUT, IF SHE wasn't "right," what could one say of Ellen Farrell, who lived in the house at the other side of us? She was one of the handsomest old women I have ever seen. In the summer and autumn evenings you could see her standing for hours at the gate of her little house, resting her right arm on the broken-down gate post, and occasionally pushing back the thin white hair from her long, bloodless, toothless face with its jutting chin and bitter mouth. Sometimes a passer-by would stop to greet her, and then the right hand on its pedestal would be used as an ear trumpet, and Ellen would shout back some savage jest. When she went out to the pub to fetch a jug of porter, she moved almost without raising her feet and this gave her what seemed a firm and stately demeanour. As she grew older, and walking became harder, she would grasp a garden railing and hang on to it for as long as it took her to recover breath, but she always held her head high, and looked angrily up the road as though she had paused only to study the view. She came from Carlow, and despised and hated Cork.

A few doors down from her lived her old husband and daughter, who were almost as odd as herself. Farrell was an old pedlar; he wore a beard and had a hump, and possessed a bit of the miraculous Knock stone that was supposed to cure all aches and pains. I was brought to him once by Mother for the cure of a recurring headache, and sure enough it went away for a day but came back again. (I was losing my sight, but nobody had noticed it.) His daughter, Annie, who was a laundress like her mother, limped because of some disease of the hip. She never went to bed at all because in her early years she had seen someone die in bed, and never cared for beds after. When she died herself, she was sitting bolt upright in the chair where she had slept for twenty years. For a period longer than that her mother had never spoken a word either to her or her father except when she shuffled by their gate in a wicked mood and snarled a curse at them. Ellen was an old woman with a long, long memory for injuries.

Yet there was a queer romance about the Farrells. They had been great supporters of Charles Stewart Parnell, and when he married a divorced woman and the priests went from door to door, threatening hell fire on anyone who voted for him, they refused to be intimidated, and Ellen even hung his portrait over the front door for the whole world to see. When the priest came to remove it, she chased him with a stick, and took an oath never again to enter a Catholic church as long as he lived. She never did, nor did her old husband, though by this time he and she had separated. Disunion in the home there might be, but not disunion about Parnell. At the same time, she continued to regard herself as a good Catholic and to pay her dues at Christmas and Easter. Once, when she had to have an official document witnessed by a clergyman, she went to Father O'Mahoney, a big, loud-voiced man whom most of the poor people were scared of. "Never saw you in my life before, my good woman," he said pompously. "Oh, yes, you did, Father," she replied with her bitter humour. "Twice a year regularly—at Christmas and Easter. However, I dare say the Protestant minister will remember me." "Give me that at once!" he shouted, but she strode scornfully away up the chapel yard and he had to run after her, snatch the document from her hand, and sign it against the church wall. "You're a very impudent old woman!" he shouted as he returned it to her. "There's a pair of us there, Father," she retorted. She was never at a loss for a dirty crack.

For six months or so after we came to Harrington's Square Mother looked after old Ellen, brought her breakfast in the morning or tea in the evening, collected her old-age pension from the post office at St. Luke's, and did whatever shopping the old woman wanted done. It wasn't much, God knows, for her house was even dirtier and barer than Grandmother's, but Mother was full of pity for her, as she was for anyone who was old or helpless or sick. Her friend, Minnie Connolly, from the other side of the square pursed her lips and shook her head over it. "I only hope she doesn't repay you the way she repaid others, Mrs. Donovan," she said. By "others," of course, she meant herself.

And, sure enough, one day when I followed my ball into Ellen's front garden, she was waiting for me behind the front door with a stick, and chased me, screaming and cursing. The honeymoon with humanity was over. Ellen had tolerated Mother rather longer than she had tolerated other specimens of the human race, but her patience could not be expected to last for ever. She even accused Mother of stealing her old-age pension! "What did I tell you, Mrs. Donovan?" asked Minnie. "The woman is bad."

She was bad, but that wasn't the worst feature of her character. She had a little house to herself, and usually there was a printed notice in the front window saying "Rooms to Let." The people she rented the rooms to were not old women of her own age but young married couples. This was in the days before council houses, and the real bait was not so much the accommodation as the prospect of permanence. The young couples, coming up the road hand in hand, knew that the old woman, leaning on her gate post, could only have a short while to live and that whoever was there when she died could not be dispossessed. And potentially it was such a nice home, with a tiny garden in front where you could grow flowers, a sitting room from which you could see everyone going by, and a back yard and toilet to yourself. Lust and hunger have no greater grip on human beings than the need for a home.

Now, there was something in the old woman that made her want young people in her house, but there was also a fiendish possessiveness and jealousy that made her realize clearly what they wanted, and no sooner had they settled in than she set herself frantically to getting rid of them. She had no scruples about what a poor, friendless old lady in her position might or might not do. First, she would lock them out at night; then she would throw away the bit of food they might have left in the kitchen; then she would scare the child from going to the back yard. If that didn't shift them, she took them to court and accused them of keeping a "bad" house or of stealing her money. Like all power maniacs, she was mad about the law, and had considerable skill in taking in magistrates. All she had to do was to put her right hand to her ear when they asked her a question and give them a witty reply. Her tenants could rarely afford a lawyer, and they probably knew that even if they won, she would continue to harass them in ways no law could control, so after dark one night you would see a donkey cart outside her gate, a small boy driving, and no light but the butt of a candle; and, taking their handful of possessions, the young people would slink back to whatever slum they had emerged from. By the time the last couple came we knew the pattern well.

8

But the most extraordinary of the neighbors was Minnie Connolly, who lived with her brother and mother, and later with her brother and his wife in the house across the square. She was a laundress, too, like her mother, and had once been maid to an old Quaker family, and while the older generation of the family lived, they were, as Minnie described it, "good to her," meaning that they sent her an occasional postal order, which, with whatever else she earned, just kept her this side of starvation. As I knew myself, the line was often indeterminate. When Mother was at work, Minnie was the only person I would stay with, and I often sat for hours in the steaming little attic where she did her laundry, and turned over the pages of the religious books of which she had a small library.

I remember with particular vividness a manuscript prayer book of which the binding had been removed. It was written in an exquisite hand—some Catholic of a hundred or so years before who had not been able to afford a printed book, or despised those he knew, had written it for his own pleasure. I confided all my ambitions to Minnie, who listened with her almost toothless mouth primmed up in amusement and replied ironically in phrases like: "Well, you don't tell me so!"

Minnie was a regular visitor to our house, and her favourite topic was priests. "Mrs. Donovan," she would say, pulling her old shawl round her as she sat on a kitchen chair in the middle of the floor, "if you were at eleven o'clock Mass yesterday, you'd never do another day's good." "Who was it?" Mother would ask, knowing that there was a good story coming. "Was it Father Tierney?" "Wisha, who else, woman?" Minnie would cry. "Himself and his ghosts!" Tierney, a white-haired, unctuous old man who saw ghosts everywhere, was more a source of interest than of edification to Minnie —not that she didn't believe in ghosts or had not had strange experiences herself, but she pooh-poohed Tierney's, and when he died, having failed to leave his money back to the Church, and no Month's Mind was said for him, it was as juicy a bit of gossip to her as if he had been found dead in the arms of one of the Holy Women. Some young English Protestant who wanted to marry a local girl had gone to Tierney for instruction, but Tierney had refused to listen to his explanations and ordered him to kneel down. The young man had told Minnie, and she did an excellent imitation of the old priest climbing a ladder to take down a large book and muttering incantations over the unfortunate boy before sending him away as wise as he had come. Later, when an attempt was made locally to get Tierney beatified, and bits of his underpants were being distributed as miraculous relics, she was savagely sarcastic about it all.

She also did excellent imitations of Sexton, the Dean in St. Patrick's Church, who gave extraordinary sermons in a thick Cork accent. Sexton, a big, rough man, did not like talking about matters of doctrine; he preferred to take his text from a new movie or a newspaper, and he leaned over the edge of the pulpit, bawling away in the voice of a market woman. "Dearly beloved brethren," he cried, "ye all saw it in the paper; the advertisement for the new film at the Coliseum. Ye all saw that it was supposed to be 'hot stuff,' and there was nothing in it at all. That is what I call deceiving the public." I have a vivid recollection of one of his sermons when an episcopal ordinance compelled him to preach on the Commandments, Sunday by Sunday. He was discussing the Second Commandment, and obviously in agony, because he felt that the Commandments were all out of date and should be scrapped. "Dearly beloved brethren," he began, "of course we're not supposed to take that seriously. Sure, we all take the Lord's name in vain. I do it myself. If I lose my temper I saw 'Ah, God damn it!' There's no harm in that at all. What the Commandment means, dearly beloved brethren, is that we shouldn't be using the Holy Name in public, the way a lot of people do. You can't go along King Street on Saturday night without hearing someone using the Holy Name. That's very bad. At the same time, there isn't any harm in that either. Sure, half the time people don't be thinking of what they're saying. But, dearly beloved brethren, if you do use it, don't use it in front of children. A child's mind is a delicate thing. A child's mind is like that marble pillar there (slapping the column beside him). It's smooth, and it doesn't hold dust nor dirt. One rub of a duster is all you need to clean that marble. A child's mind is like marble. Don't roughen it." I thought it the best sermon I had ever heard, and I liked Sexton and his rough-neck oratory, but neither Mother nor Minnie could tolerate it. Minnie did a first-class imitation of him, preaching on the text that "Not a bird shall fall" and announcing in scandalized tones that it was "all nonsense—my goodness, they're falling by thousands all over the world every minute." She had her crow over Sexton as well, when an impostor who called himself the "Crown Prince of Abyssinia" served his Mass and reviewed the troops before the police caught up on him.

After religion—a long way after religion—she loved novelettes, and these she brought to Mother and discussed them as though they were police court reports. I don't think it ever once crossed her mind—which in some ways was so profound—that they might not be literally true. "Ah, woman," she would cry impatiently with a hasty flick of her skinny arm, "sure he was a fool to have anything to do with a girl like that. Do you mean to tell me that he couldn't see for himself the sort of girl she was?" I fancy that she had a great interest in the passions, because she had quite an attachment to the Bad Girl of the neighborhood and though she would anyway have tried to have an influence for good on the girl and protect her from the Holy Women, she seemed to love hearing about married men and jealous wives and officers from the barrack. She would stride hastily into our kitchen, clutching the shawl or old coat about her as though she were cold, her head bowed, but with a little smile on her thick negroid lips. "Wisha, wait till you hear what's after happening, ma'am," she would cry modestly. "You'll never be the better of it." (For some reason, that and "You'll never do a day's good" were her blurbs for the dust jacket of some new romance.) Then, for an hour or more you got the whole story as if it were a novelette. "But if he did not feel that way towards her, Mrs. Donovan," she would cry dramatically, letting her hand fall on Mother's knee while she looked up from under her thick brows with a penetrating glance, "why did he use those particular words?"

Minnie had an extraordinarily striking face, with a high forehead, high cheekbones and sunken, dreaming eyes, thick poet's lips and a toothless mouth. She shuffled hastily about the locality in some foot-gear that never seemed to fit, clutching her ragged old coat across her breast and with her head well down till she recognized someone she liked, and then it would be suddenly raised to reveal the most enchanting smile in the world. I do not think I am exaggerating. Sometimes it comes before me in the early hours of the morning, and it seems as though all the suffering and delight of humanity were in that one strange smile. Minnie had spent some time in the Big House, as she euphemistically called the Lunatic Asylum, and someone once told me that while she was there she wept almost without ceasing. The doctors called it acute melancholia, but what does melancholia mean, and what do the majority of doctors know about people of Minnie's quality? Whatever it was, it had left no trace on her character, except when she saw suffering inflicted on an animal, and then she seemed to go off her head; screamed in the middle of the street and stamped off to complain to the police or the Society for the Prevention of Cruelty to Animals. They, of course, knew that she was only an old maid and had spent some time in the Lunatic Asylum and so they paid little heed to her.

Yet that woman who had been in the asylum was one of the sanest women I have ever met, and probably the finest. Sometimes when I think of her I seem to see her holding a starving dog or a poisoned cat, talking to it gently, her whole face lit up, and I realize how vulgar are all the pictures we see of the Good Shepherd. Wherever there was sickness or death, there would come the knock, and Minnie would be outside the door in her ragged old coat, asking in her expressionless voice: "Is there anything I can do for you, ma'am?" ready to scrub or cook or nurse or pray; to hold the hand of some dying man in hers or to wash his poor dirty body when the life had gone from him. If someone offered her sixpence or a shilling, she was too humble to refuse it, unless it was someone as poor as herself, and then she pushed it away with a smile and said dryly: "You'll be wanting that yourself, ma'am," though what she was rejecting might be her own dinner for the day. When I grew up and realized that the woman I had known was a saint I understood something of her demonic pride and her terrible abnegation. At the best of times she must have been a cruelly difficult woman to get on with, for though she and Mother adored one another, and up to the day of Minnie's death Mother shared whatever few shillings she had with her, there were long spells of not speaking, and Minnie would not glance at the side of the road Mother was on, and Mother was as hurt as a schoolgirl.

As I say, she had a passion for novelettes which she fed to poor Mother, who, though she could never resist a love story, no matter how bad, or deny a tear to suffering virtue, had a natural distinction of taste. I suspect that Minnie had no taste, but she had a fierce, combative masculine intellect, which, if it had

106

been trained, might have made her a formidable logician or philosopher, and she would have had no hesitation about telling the pope himself where he went wrong. What she really enjoyed about a sermon was when a priest made a fool of himself about some matter of doctrine. "Heresy, ma'am, plain heresy!" she would say flatly. "St. Ignatius Loyola distinctly lays it down." I am sure it was she who told Mother that the Church was going to hell with all the vulgarians who were being raised to the altars, and I seem to remember one angry speech of hers on the subject in which she contrasted Teresa of Avila with some modern saint —probably Thérèse of Lisieux, who from Minnie's point of view would be only a stage-struck child. The great Teresa would have had no difficulty at all in placing Minnie Connolly.

9

GERTIE, ELLEN, AND MINNIE had very different fates. So far as Gertie was concerned, it all happened as in a story-book. One winter night, the *Hannibal* went down with all hands. Gertie got the lump sum, and as she had always known she would, she left Cork for London to open a superior lodging house. I remember her bouncing with glee and confidence when she came in to say good-bye, and I remember that to my astonishment both my parents seemed sorry to lose her. They too had become used to that flaming parakeet of a woman, and I think they suddenly realized that without her their lives would be poorer and less interesting.

Ellen Farrell's was different but equally characteristic. One day there arrived at her house a newly married couple, of which the young husband would strike pity into anyone's heart, he was so guileless and gentle. He was so unsure of himself in the part of husband and father that he talked to kids like myself as equals and called all the other married men "Sir," an example of modesty that made Father his slave for life. He loved coming to his door in shirt sleeves and carrying on conversations with Father and the man in the house at the other side, and in the evenings he dug the little front garden.

Within a few weeks Ellen was on the war-path again. She locked the front door on him, and he got in through the bedroom window. She did it again and he started to break down the front door. By this time Father was beginning to see that his politeness was not obsequiousness and to say approvingly that he was "no balk." When the plants began to take root in the front garden, Ellen poured buckets of red-hot cinders on them. He didn't seem in the least put out. He affected to believe that the plants only needed water and dragged buckets of it from the back yard, spilling each one in the kitchen as though by accident till he flooded the old woman out. She took him to court, but he defended himself, and the magistrate, beginning at last to get suspicious of the bonneted old lady with the amusing tongue, decided in his favour. There was great rejoicing in the neighborhood. Ellen shouted defiantly as she left the court; "The Corkies has me bet at last." To the end she remained a loyal Carlow woman.

But it was not in her to admit that she really was defeated. She would remain for weeks in sullen silence, and then remember that when she was dead, the lodgers would be growing flowers in her front garden, and children would be playing about her fireplace, and then she would start to curse them, sullenly and bitterly, leaning on her gate post with her hand to her ear, her grey hair blowing in the wind. The young husband with his sly humour would intercept the occasional letters that reached her and re-address them to "The Beautiful Mrs. Ellen Farrell," or "Ellen, the Tinker from Carlow, Cork."

My memory of her end is uncertain, but I have a strong impression that it was Minnie Connolly who came to look after her when she was dying. It was certainly Minnie who wrote to the old woman's second daughter, who was married to a baker in the French provinces. The hunchback husband and crippled daughter came and sat for hours in the bare kitchen downstairs, waiting for her to speak the word of reconciliation, but she only spat when their presence was mentioned. She was so deaf that her confession could be heard all over the terrace. She still retained her savage humour, and agreed to forgive all her enemies, but made an exception of Parnell's successor, John Redmond, because, she maintained, she had it on the best authority that he had betrayed Ireland. The Catholic Church is wonderfully tolerant of political vagaries like that, and the exception was allowed to pass. Maybe the priest did not think much of John Redmond himself.

Minnie Connolly is probably astonished if she knows that the solemn little boy who read prayer books in her attic bedroom while she ironed remembers her as a myth, a point in history at which the whole significance of human life seems to be concentrated, rather as Ellen Farrell thought of Parnell. She would be still more astonished at the company she keeps, but what she had in common with Gertie Twomey and Ellen Farrell was that each of them knew exactly where she was going. Ellen was going to Hell, or wherever it is people go who think only of themselves. Minnie was going to Heaven, if that is the right name for the place where people go who think only of poisoned cats and starving dogs and dying people. Gertie, of course, was merely going to London.

III

GO WHERE GLORY
WAITS THEE

10

FOR KIDS LIKE MYSELF social life was represented by the shop-front and the gas-lamp.
This was mainly because we could rarely bring other
kids home in the evenings; the houses were too small,
and after the fathers came home from work, children
became a nuisance. Besides, most families had something to hide; if it wasn't an old grandmother like mine
or a father who drank, it was how little they had to eat.
This was always a matter of extreme delicacy, and the
ultimate of snobbery was expressed for us by the loud
woman up the road who was supposed to call her son
in from play with: "Tommy, come in to your tea, toast
and two eggs!"

But as well as that, there was a sort of fever in
the blood that mounted towards evening. After tea, you

would hear the children whistling and calling from every direction, on a falling note: "SU-sie! JOHNnie!" at least those of them whose parents did not set them at once to their homework; and then by some immemorial instinct they would begin to converge like wild animals or savages from the jungle of the streets on the campfires of the shop-windows that glowed warmly in the cold evenings. The shopkeepers didn't like these gatherings at all because they gave their shops a bad name, and now and then one would come out and clap her hands and cry: "Let ye be going home now, children! This is no place for ye at this hour of night." But the children would rarely go farther than the nearest lamp-post and after a while they would drift back to the shop-front until their mothers' voices began to fill the night with names uttered on a rising note: "SuSIE!" or "JohnNIE!"

The shop-fronts and gas-lamps were quite as exclusive as city clubs. The boys from our neighborhood usually gathered outside Miss Murphy's shop at the foot of the Square, while the respectable boys of the Ballyhooley Road—the children of policemen, minor officials, and small shopkeepers—gathered outside Miss Long's by the Quarry. I lived in a sort of social vacuum between the two, for though custom summoned me to Miss Murphy's with boys of my own class who sometimes went without boots and had no ambition to be educated, my instinct summoned me to Miss Long's and the boys who wore boots and got educated whether they liked it or not.

As nothing would persuade Father but that he was a home-loving body, nothing would persuade me but that I belonged to a class to which boots and education came natural. I was always very sympathetic with children in the story-books I read who had been kidnapped by tramps and gipsies, and for a lot of the time I was inclined to think that something like that must have happened to myself. Apart from any natural liking I may have had for education, I knew it was the only way of escaping from the situation in which I found myself. Everyone admitted that. They said you could get nowhere without education. They blamed their own failure in life on the lack of it. They talked of it as Father talked of the valuable bits of machinery he had stored on top of the wardrobe, as something that would be bound to come in handy in seven years time.

The difficulty was to get started. It seemed to be extremely hard to get an education, or even—at the level on which we lived—to discover what it was. There was a little woman up the road called Mrs. Busteed whose elder son was supposed to be the most brilliant boy in Ireland, and I watched him enviously on his way to and from the North Monastery, but his mother had been a stewardess on the boats and it was always said that "they made great money on the boats." Of course, education implied nice manners instead of coarse ones—I could see that for myself when I contrasted Mother's manners with those of my father's family—and I was a polite and considerate boy most of the time, except when the business of getting an education proved too much for me, and I had to go to Confession and admit that I had again been disobedient and disrespectful to my parents—about the only sin I ever got the chance of committing till I was fifteen.

So I was drawn to the policemen's sons and the others on the Ballyhooley Road who produced all those signs of a proper education that I had learned to recognize from the boys' weeklies I read. One boy might have a bicycle, another a stamp album; they had a real football instead of the raggy ball that I kicked round or a real cricket bat with wickets; and occasionally I saw one with a copy of the *Boy's Own Paper,* which cost sixpence and had half-tone illustrations instead of the papers that I read, which cost a penny and had only line drawings.

Between those two groups I felt very lonely and unwelcome. Those who frequented them must have thought me a freak—the poorer kids because I spoke in what probably sounded like an affected accent, and used strange words and phrases that I had picked up from my reading; the others because I was only an intruder from the shop-front where I belonged, try-ing to force his company on them. The only one of them I became really acquainted with was Willie Curtin, whose family kept a florist's shop in which he did messages. He was a lame lad with a long, pale, handsome, desperate face and a loud, boisterous voice, who smoked cigarette butts by the score and broke in defiantly on any group, pushing people aside with his arms like a swimmer. Like myself, he read endlessly, and he ate whatever he was reading right down to the type—a habit I detested because I treasured every-thing I read. We carried on complicated swaps, which with Willie were always complicated further by con-siderations like a foreign coin or a magic-lantern slide. I envied him his warm welcome for himself, and it wasn't until long after that I guessed he was really a lame, lonely, neglected boy who also did not belong anywhere.

That was probably why we both read so much, but whereas Willie read indiscriminately, I had a strong preference for school stories and above all for the penny weeklies, the *Gem* and the *Magnet.* Their appeal for me was that the characters in them were getting a really good education, and that some of it was bound to brush off on me. All the same, a really good education like that demanded a great many things I did not have, like an old fellow who didn't drink and an old one who didn't work, an uncle with a racing car who would give me a tip of five pounds to blow on a feed in the dormitory after lights out, long trousers, a short jacket and a top hat, bicycles, footballs, and cricket bats. For this I should need a rich relative in the States, and we were short of relatives in the States. The only one I could get certain tidings of was a patrolman in the Chicago Police known as "Big Tim" Fahy. He was a cousin of Mother, and such a giant that even Father, who was a six-footer, said he felt like a small boy beside him. Tim's only ambition was to join the Royal Irish Constabulary, where height was as well regarded as it had been in the court of Frederick the Great, but one day in the "Western Star" pub, six English soldiers had jeered him about his height, and he had thrown the whole six into the street. The police had been sent for, and he had thrown them after the soldiers. And that was the end of Tim's ambition, for no one with a conviction against him would be accepted in the R.I.C. Murphy's Brewery had offered him a handsome job as sandwichman to illustrate what Murphy's stout did for you, but he was too proud for a job like that, so he emigrated. He was famous enough in Chicago, to judge by the newspaper clippings the Fahys showed us when we visited them, and we had a photograph of him on the sideboard, wearing a sword, but I didn't know if even he could afford to send me to a school like those I read about.

So I adored education from afar, and strove to be worthy of it, as later I adored beautiful girls and strove to be worthy of them, and with similar results. I played cricket with a raggy ball and an old board hacked into shape for a bat before a wicket chalked on some dead wall. I kept in training by shadow boxing before the mirror in the kitchen, and practised the deadly straight left with which the hero knocked out the bully of the school. I even adopted the public-school code for my own, and did not tell lies, or inform on other boys, or yell when I was beaten. It wasn't easy, because the other fellows did tell lies, and told on one another in the most shameless way, and, when they were beaten, yelled that their wrists were broken and even boasted later of their own cleverness, and when I behaved in the simple, manly way recommended in the school stories, they said I was mad or that I was "shaping" (the Cork word for swanking), and even the teachers seemed to regard it as an impertinence.

I was always very fond of heights, and afterwards it struck me that reading was only another form of height, and a more perilous one. It was a way of looking beyond your own back yard into the neighbours'. Our back yard had a high wall, and by early afternoon it made the whole kitchen dark, and when the evening was fine, I climbed the door of the outhouse and up the roof to the top of the wall. It was on a level with the respectable terrace behind ours, which had front gardens and a fine view, and I often sat there for hours on terms of relative equality with the policeman in the first house who dug close beside me and gave me ugly looks but could not think up a law to keep me from sitting on my own back wall. From this I could see Gardiner's Hill falling headlong to the valley of the city, with its terraces of tall houses and its crest of dark trees. It was all lit up when our little house was already in darkness. In the mornings, the first thing I did when I got up was to mount a chair under the attic window and push up the window-frame to see the same hillside when it was still in shadow and its colours had the stiffness of early-morning light. I have a distinct recollection of climbing out the attic window and, after negotiating the peril of the raised window-frame, crawling up the roof to the ridge to enlarge my field of view, but Mother must have caught me at this, because I do not remember having done it often.

Then there was the quarry that fell sheer from the neighborhood of the barrack to the Ballyhooley Road. It was a noisome place where people dumped their rubbish and gangs of wild kids had stoning matches after school and poor people from the lanes poked among the rubbish for spoil, but I ignored them and picked my way through the discarded bully-beef tins and climbed to some ledge of rock or hollow in the quarry face, and sat there happily, surveying the whole neighbourhood from Mayfield Chapel, which crowned the hillside on the edge of the open country, to the spire of Saint Luke's Church below me, and below that again, in the distance was the River Lee with its fun- nels and masts, and the blue hills over it. Immediately beneath me was the Ballyhooley Road, winding up the hill from Saint Luke's Cross, with its little houses and their tiny front gardens, and (on the side nearest me) the back yards where the women came to peg up their washing; and all the time the shadow moved with a chill you could feel, and the isolated spots of sunlight contracted and their colour deepened. I felt like some sort of wild bird, secure from everything and observing everything—the horse and cart coming up the road, the little girl with her skipping rope on the pavement, or the old man staggering by on his stick—all of them unconscious of the eagle eye that watched them.

But whatever the height, whether that of story-book or quarry, the eagle had to descend. Up there I was cold and hungry, and the loneliness and the longing for society made me feel even worse. Mother would soon be finished work. At some houses she did half a day, which ended about three o'clock and for which she was paid ninepence, and at others a whole day that did not end until six or later and for which she was paid one and sixpence. Depending on the humour of the mistress or maid she worked for, I might be allowed to call for her a little before she finished work, and in one house in Tivoli, beside the river, where the maid—Ellie Mahoney—was also an orphan from the Good Shepherd Orphanage, I was not only admitted to the big, warm area kitchen after school and given my tea, but, if the family was out, I was allowed to accompany Mother upstairs while she did the bedrooms, or go to the lumber room in the attic which was chock full of treasures—old pamphlets, guide books, phrase books in French and German, school books, including a French primer, old dance programmes from Vienna and Munich that contained musical illustrations of Schubert's songs, and—greatest prize of all—an illustrated book of the Oberammergau Passion Play with the text in German and English. It was junk that would have meant nothing to anyone else, but for me it was "the right twigs for an eagle's nest," and, seeing my passion for it, Ellie Mahoney soon cleared it out and let me have my pick. It filled my mind with images of how educated people lived; the places they saw, the things they did, and the lordly way they spoke to hotel managers and railway porters, disputing the bill, checking the two trunks and five bags that were to go on the express to Cologne, and tipping right, left, and centre.

It was only another aspect of the vision I caught in the master bedrooms that overlooked the railway line and the river. There were triptych mirrors, silver-handled brushes with engraved designs, and curiously shaped bottles that contained oil and scents and with which I experimented recklessly when Mother's back was turned. Sometimes, since then, whenever I stay in such a house, I wonder what really goes on when I am not looking; what small black face has studied itself in the mirror of the dressing table, or what grubby little paw has plied the silver-handled brushes and poured on the bay rum, and I turn round expecting to see a tiny figure dash recklessly down the stairs to the safety of the kitchen. For these were dangerous heights, and sometimes I became so fascinated by a passing boat or a lighted train on its way down to Queenstown between the roadway and the house that I failed to notice someone crossing the railway bridge from the river road till I heard the bell jangle below in the kitchen, and took the stairs three or four at a time, almost knocking down Ellie as she trotted up, nervously arranging her starched cap.

Ellie was typical of the orphan children—a thin, desiccated, anxious old maid with tiny, red-rimmed eyes, a little scrap of grey hair screwed up under her old-fashioned cap, and a tinny, tormented voice. But her heart was full of girlish passion, and she loved to discuss with Mother whether or not she should accept the proposal of the milkman, who was now becoming pressing. Ellie's wages, as I remember distinctly over all the years, were five shillings a week, but I fancy that in her forty-odd years of service she had managed to put by a few pounds, and with her little dowry and her blameless character, considered herself an eligible partner for a settled man like the milkman. At least, as she said, she would have someone to look after her in her old age. I think this must have been something of a dream to the orphan girls, because Mother caused me fierce pangs of jealousy when she told me that she had prayed for a girl—someone who would look after her in her old age. But, instead of marrying the milkman, Ellie contracted lupus, and while her poor little face was being eaten away, Mother (and, of course, I) visited her regularly in the Incurable Hospital on the Wellington Road, and until the end she continued to congratulate herself on having had employers who did not throw her into the workhouse to die. I was sorry when she did die and I saw her laid out for burial with a white linen cloth covering her demolished face, because I had planned everything differently, and had arranged with Mother (and I suspect with Ellie herself) that when I made a fortune she would come as maid to us, and be paid a really substantial wage— I think I had fixed it at seven shillings a week.

So I scampered down the quarry face to the snug, suburban road with its gas-lamps and smooth pavements, and waited by the tram stop at Saint Luke's Cross where I could be sure Mother would not escape me. I would feel guilty because I knew I should have stayed at home and lit the fire so that she would not have to re-light it after a hard day's work, but I hated to be in the house alone. I sat in the dusk on the high wall overlooking the church, afraid to look back for fear I might grow dizzy and fall, and when a tram came wheezing up the hill from town I followed the men who got off it in quest of cigarette pictures. Sometimes she would have only her wages, but occasionally a maid would give her a bit of cold meat or a slice of apple pie for my supper. Sometimes, too, we would have the house to ourselves, and we would light the

fire and sit beside it in the darkness, and she would
tell me stories or sing songs with me. These were almost always Moore's Melodies. A whole generation has
grown up that has what seems to me an idiotic attitude
to "Tommy" Moore, as it calls him in its supercilious
way—mainly, because it has never learned to sing
him. His songs were the only real education that the
vast majority of Irish people got during the nineteenth
century and after, even if it was an education of the
heart, of which we all had too much, rather than an
education of the intelligence, of which we had too
little. My own favourites were "Farewell, but Whenever You Welcome the Hour" and "How Dear to Me the
Hour When Daylight Dies." I took the songs I sang with
a deadly literalness that sometimes reduced me to sobs,
and with the paternal melancholia I loved songs of
twilight like "Those Evening Bells" (a choice which, I
subsequently learned, I shared with the great actor
Edmund Kean). But Mother was very fond of "I Saw
from the Beach," and I can still remember the feeling
of slight jealousy and mortification that possessed me
when she sang:

Ne'er tell me of glories, serenely adorning
   The close of our day, the calm eve of our night;—
Give me back, give me back the wild freshness of
      Morning,
Her clouds and her tears are worth Evening's best
      light.

As I say, I took things literally, and it seemed to
me as if she were appealing to some happiness she had
known in youth of which I was not a part, but she
made it up to me by singing her own favourite, "Go
Where Glory Waits Thee," and I put up with the dull

tune for the sake of the words that seemed to be addressed to myself.

> *Go where glory waits thee,*
> *But, while fame elates thee,*
>   *Oh! still remember me.*
> *When the praise thou meetest*
> *To thine ear is sweetest,*
>   *Oh! then remember me.*

But often it was misery to return from the
heights, and I shuddered at the difference between
the two worlds, the world in my head and the world
that really existed. The fever in my blood would drive
me out of the kitchen, where I had been reading or
singing Moore's Melodies to the clublike atmosphere
of the pool of light outside the shop-window, and everything would go well for a few minutes till I said something wrong or used a word that no one understood,
and then the whole group jeered me, and called me
"Molly" (our word for "sissy") and later "Foureyes," and
I realized that once again I had been talking the language of the heights, which the others did not speak,
and that they thought me mad. Sometimes I didn't
know but that I was mad.

The trouble was that I was always a little bit of
what I had picked up from book or song or picture or
glimpse of some different sort of life, always half in
and half out of the world of reality, like Moses de-
scending the mountain or a dreamer waking. Once
I had read about Robin Hood, I had to make myself a
bow out of a bamboo curtain rod and practise archery
in the Square. Going along the street, remembering
Chopin's Funeral March, I was never just a small boy
remembering a piece of music; I was, like any other
imaginative boy, everything from the corpse to the

brass band and the firing party. When I induced a couple of younger boys to assist me at cricket and stood with a home-made bat before a wicket chalked on a wall, I was always the Dark Horse of the school, emerging to save its honour when all seemed lost, and I even stood my ground when a policeman came stalking towards us, and the "school" took to its heels round the nearest corner.

"What do you mean playing ball on the public street?" the policeman asked angrily.

"Excuse me, this is not a public street," I replied firmly. "This square is private property."

That day the bobby was so stunned at being cheeked by a small spectacled boy with an imitation bat that I got away with it, but most of the time I didn't get away with it. I got in trouble for being cheeky when I was only acting out a part and was called a liar when I was still half in, half out of the dream and only telling the truth as best I could.

It was still worse when I interfered to prevent what I thought an injustice. This was more than mere imitation of the head boy of the school, more even than the gentle nostalgic sentiment of Moore applied to a half-barbarous society—it was the natural reaction of a mother's boy who knew what suffering and injustice really were, but it was more dangerous, because the one thing a Sir Galahad needs is a more than theoretical knowledge of the Noble Art of Self-Defence. Sometimes surprise was enough, as it was sometimes enough for Minnie Connolly when she bawled at a brutal carter, but often it was not, and before ever I got in the deadly straight left I had developed from shadow boxing before the mirror, I got a knee in the groin or a kick in the shin or had my glasses knocked off, and went home, weeping and determined that for the future I would carry a Chinese dagger, preferably poisoned.

And yet I could not help brooding on injustice, and making a fool of myself about it. I must have been several years older when I heard that a young fellow I knew—a wild, handsome boy whose father beat him savagely—had run away from home and was being searched for by the police. The story was told in whispers. He would be picked up and sent to a reformatory. That evening I found him myself, lurking in an alleyway, his long face dirty with tears, and tried to make him come home with me. He wouldn't, and I could not leave him there like that, lonely and lost and crying. I made it clear that I would stay with him, and at last he agreed to return home if I went with him and pleaded for him. When I knocked at the door he stood against the wall, his hands in his pockets and his head bent. His elder sister opened the door, and I made my little speech, and she promised to see that he wasn't punished. Then I went home in a glow of self-righteousness, feeling that I had saved him from the fate I had always dreaded myself. I felt sure he would be grateful, and that from this out we would be good friends, but it didn't happen like that at all. When we met again he would not look at me; instead, he turned away with a sneer, and I knew his father had beaten him again, and that it was all my fault. As a protector of the weak, I was never worth a damn.

CHRISTMAS WAS ALWAYS the worst time of the year for me, though it began well, weeks before Christmas itself, with the Christmas numbers. Normally I read only boys' weeklies, but at this time of year all papers, juvenile and adult, seemed equally desirable, as though the general magic of the season transcended the particular magic of any one paper. School stories, detective stories, and adventure stories all merged into one great Christmas story.

Christmas numbers were, of course, double numbers; their pale-green and red covers suddenly bloomed into glossy colours, with borders of red-berried holly. Even their titles dripped with snow. As for the pictures within, they showed roads under snow, and old houses under snow, with diamond-paned windows that were brilliant in the darkness. I never knew what magic there was in snow for me because in Ireland we rarely saw it for more than two or three days in the year, and that was usually in the late spring. In real life it meant little to me except that Father—who was always trying to make a manly boy of me as he believed himself to have been at my age—made me wash my face and hands in it to avert chilblains. I think its magic in the Christmas numbers depended on the contrast between it and the Christmas candles, the holly branches with the red berries, the log fires, and the gleaming windows. It was the contrast between light and dark, life and death; the cold and darkness that reigned when Life came into the world. Going about her work, Mother would suddenly break into song:

> *Natum videte*
> *Regem angelorum* . . .

and I would join in. It was the season of imagination. My trouble was that I already had more than my share of imagination.

Then there were no more Christmas numbers, but I managed to preserve the spirit of them, sitting at my table with pencil and paper, trying to draw Christmas scenes of my own—dark skies and walls, bright snow and windows. When I was older and could trace figures, these turned into the figures of the manger scene, cut out and mounted on cardboard to make a proper crib.

Christmas Eve was the culmination of this season, the day when the promise of the Christmas numbers should be fulfilled. The shops already had their green and red streamers, and in the morning Mother decorated the house with holly and ivy. Much as I

longed for it, we never had red-berried holly, which
cost more. The Christmas candle, two feet high and
a couple of inches thick, was set in a jam crock,
wrapped in coloured paper, and twined about with
holly. Everything was ready for the feast. For a lot of
the day I leaned against the front door or wandered
slowly down the road to the corner, trying to appear
careless and indifferent so that no one should know I
was really waiting for the postman. Most of the Christmas mail we got came on Christmas Eve, and though I
don't think I ever got a present through the post,
that did not in the least diminish my expectations of
one. Whatever experience might have taught me, the
Christmas numbers taught differently.

Father had a half-day on Christmas Eve, and
came home at noon with his week's pay in his pocket
—that is, when he got home at all. Mother and I
knew well how easily he was led astray by out-of-works
who waited at the street corners for men in regular
jobs, knowing that on Christmas Eve no one could
refuse them a pint. But I never gave that aspect of it
much thought. It wasn't for anything so commonplace
as Father's weekly pay that I was waiting. I even ignored the fact that when he did come in, there was
usually an argument and sometimes a quarrel. At ordinary times when he did not give Mother enough to pay
the bills, she took it with resignation, and if there was
a row it was he who provoked it by asking: "Well, isn't
that enough for you?" But at Christmas she would
fight and fight desperately. One Christmas Eve he
came home and handed her the housekeeping money
with a complacent air, and she looked at the coins in
her hand and went white. "Lord God, what am I to do
with that?" I heard her whisper despairingly, and I
listened in terror because she never invoked the name

of God. Father suddenly blew up into the fury he had been cooking up all the way home—a poor, hard-working man deprived of his little bit of pleasure at Christmas time because of an extravagant wife and child. "Well, what do you want it for?" he snarled. "What do I want it for?" she asked distractedly, and went through her shopping list, which, God knows, must have been modest enough. And then he said something that I did not understand, and I heard her whispering in reply and there was a frenzy in her voice that I would not have believed possible; "Do you think I'll leave him without it on the one day of the year?"

Years later I suddenly remembered the phrase because of its beauty, and realized that it was I who was to be left without a toy, and on this one day of the year that seemed to her intolerable. And yet I did not allow it to disturb me; I had other expectations, and I was very happy when the pair of us went shopping together, down Blarney Lane, past the shop in the big old house islanded in Goulnaspurra, where they sold the coloured cardboard cribs I coveted, with shepherds and snow, manger and star, and across the bridge to Myles's Toy Shop on the North Main Street. There in the rainy dusk, jostled by prams and drunken women in shawls, and thrust on one side by barefooted children from the lanes, I stood in wonder, thinking which treasure Santa Claus would bring me from the ends of the earth to show his appreciation of the way I had behaved in the past twelve months. As he was a most superior man, and I a most superior child, I saw no limit to the possibilities of the period, and no reason why Mother should not join in my speculations.

It was usually dark when we tramped home together, up Wyse's Hill, from which we saw the whole

132

city lit up beneath us and the trams reflected in the water under Patrick's Bridge; or later—when we lived in Barrackton, up Summerhill, Mother carrying the few scraps of meat and the plum pudding from Thompson's and me something from the Penny Bazaar. We had been out a long time, and I was full of expectations of what the postman might have brought in the meantime. Even when he hadn't brought anything, I didn't allow myself to be upset, for I knew that the poor postmen were dreadfully overworked at this time of year. And even if he didn't come later, there was always the final Christmas-morning delivery. I was an optimistic child, and the holly over the mirror in the kitchen and the red paper in the lighted window of the huxter shop across the street assured me that the Christmas numbers were right and anything might happen.

There were lesser pleasures to look forward to, like the lighting of the Christmas candle and the cutting of the Christmas cake. As the youngest of the household I had the job of lighting the candle and saying solemnly: "The light of Heaven to our souls on the last day," and Mother's principal worry was that before the time came Father might slip out to the pub and spoil the ritual, for it was supposed to be carried out by the oldest and the youngest, and Father, by convention, was the oldest, though, in fact, as I later discovered, he was younger than Mother.

In those days the cake and candle were supposed to be presented by the small shop-keeper from whom we bought the tea, sugar, paraffin oil, and so on. We could not afford to shop in the big stores where everything was cheaper, because they did not give credit to poor people, and most of the time we lived on credit. But each year our "presents" seemed to grow smaller,

and Mother would comment impatiently on the mean-
ness of Miss O' or Miss Mac in giving us a tiny candle
or a stale cake. (When the 1914 War began they
stopped giving us the cake.) Mother could never believe that people could be so mean, but where we were
concerned, they seemed to be capable of anything.
The lighted candle still left me with two expectations.
However late it grew I never ceased to expect the
postman's knock, and even when that failed, there was
the certainty that Christmas Morning would set everything right.

But when I woke on Christmas Morning, I felt the
season of imagination slipping away from me and the
world of reality breaking in. If all Santa Claus could
bring me from the North Pole was something I could
have bought in Myles's Toy Shop for a couple of pence,
he seemed to me to be wasting his time. Then the
postman came, on his final round before a holiday that
already had begun to seem eternal, and either he
brought nothing for us, or else he brought the dregs
of the Christmas mail, like a Christmas card from
somebody who had just got Mother's card and remembered her existence at the last moment. Often, even
this would be in an unsealed envelope and it would upset her for hours. It was strange in a woman to whom
a penny was money that an unsealed envelope seemed
to her the worst of ill-breeding, equivalent to the small
candle or the stale cake—not a simple measure of
economy, but plain, unadulterated bad taste.

Comparing Christmas gifts with other kids didn't
take long or give much satisfaction, and even then the
day was overshadowed by the harsh rule that I was
not supposed to call at other children's houses or they
at mine. This, Mother said, was the family season,
which was all very well for those who had families

but death to an only child. It was the end of the season
of imagination, and there was no reason to think it
would ever come again. Nothing had happened as it
happened in the Christmas numbers. There was no
snow; no relative had returned from the States with
presents for everyone; there was nothing but Christmas Mass and the choir thundering out *Natum videte
regem angelorum* as though they believed it, when any
fool could see that things were just going on in the
same old way. Mother would sigh and say: "I never
believe it's really Christmas until I hear the *Adeste,*"
but if that was all that Christmas meant to her she
was welcome to it. Most Christmas days I could have
screamed with misery. I argued with Mother that other
kids were just as depressed as I was, and dying to see
me, but I never remember that she allowed me to
stray far from the front door.

But, bad as Christmas Day was, St. Stephen's Day
was terrible. It needed no imagination, only as much
as was required to believe that you really had a dead
wren on the holly bush you carried from door to door,
singing:

> *I up with me stick and I gave him a fall,*
> *And I brought him here to visit ye all.*

Father was very contemptuous, watching this,
and took it as another sign of the disappearance of
youthful manliness, for in his young days not only did
they wash their faces in snow, but on Christmas Day
they raised the countryside with big sticks, killing
wrens—or droleens, as we called them. Everyone knew
that it was the droleen's chirping that had alerted the
Roman soldiers in the Garden of Gethsemane and
pointed out to them where Christ was concealed, and
in Father's young days they had carried it around with

great pomp, all the mummers disguised. It seemed to him positively indecent to ask for money on the strength of a dead wren that you didn't have. It wasn't the absence of the wren that worried Mother, even if he was an informer, for she adored birds and supported a whole regiment of them through the winter, but the fear that I would be a nuisance to other women as poor as herself who didn't have a penny to give the wren boys.

In the afternoon she and I went to see the cribs in the chapels. (There were none in the parish churches.) She was never strong enough to visit the seven cribs you had to visit to get the special blessing, but we always went to the chapel of the Good Shepherd Convent in Sunday's Well where she had gone to school. She was very loyal to those she called "the old nuns," the nuns who had been kind to her when she was a child.

One Christmas Santa Claus brought me a toy engine. As it was the only present I had received, I took it with me to the convent, and played with it on the floor while Mother and "the old nuns" discussed old times and how much nicer girls used to be then. But it was a young nun who brought us in to see the crib. When I saw the Holy Child in the manger I was very distressed, because little as I had, he had nothing at all. For me it was fresh proof of the incompetence of Santa Claus—an elderly man who hadn't even remembered to give the Infant Jesus a toy and who should have been retired long ago. I asked the young nun politely if the Holy Child didn't like toys, and she replied composedly enough: "Oh, he does, but his mother is too poor to afford them." That settled it. My mother was poor too, but at Christmas she at least managed to buy me something, even if it was only a box of crayons. I distinctly remember getting into the crib and putting the engine between his outstretched arms. I probably showed him how to wind it as well, because a small baby like that would not be clever enough to know. I remember too the tearful feeling of reckless generosity with which I left him there in the nightly darkness of the chapel, clutching my toy engine to his chest.

Because somehow I knew even then exactly how that child felt—the utter despondency of realizing that he had been forgotten and that nobody had brought him anything; the longing for the dreary, dreadful holidays to pass till his father got to hell out of the house, and the postman returned again with the promise of better things.

12

THE PRINCIPAL DIFFICULTY about the world in my head was that there seemed to be no connection at all between the idea of education I formed from the boys' weeklies and education as it was practised in the schools I knew. There was the boys' school at St. Luke's, for example, where the headmaster was called Downey, a fierce, red, sweaty bull of a man with a white moustache, a bald head he was for ever wiping with a huge white handkerchief, and a long cane that he flourished joyously. The boys had a song about him that was probably first sung about an Elizabethan schoolmaster, but it fitted him perfectly:

> *Tommy is a holy man,*
> *He goes to Mass on Sunday,*

Go Where Glory Waits Thee

*He prays to God to give him strength
To slap the boys on Monday.*

This was probably true, because he combined the sanctimoniousness of a reformed pirate with the brutality of a half-witted drill sergeant. With him the cane was never a mere weapon; it was a real extension of his personality, like a musician's instrument or a ventriloquist's dummy—something you could imagine his bringing home with him and reaching out for in the middle of the night as a man reaches out for his wife or his bottle. He was a real artist with it, and with his fat, soft, sexual fingers he caressed your hand into the exact position at which a cut would cause the most excruciating pain. He sent the boys out for canes on approval, and tested them carefully, swishing them and peering at them with his small piggy eyes for flaws that would be invisible to anyone else, and when one of them broke in his hand, as happened occasionally when he was flogging some slow child about the bare legs, one glance was enough for him to size up the possibilities of the two pieces so that he could carry on the job with the more formidable one. When, in those odd moments of recollection that afflict the most conscientious of men, he stood at the front door and looked out at the spring sunshine with a puzzled frown, as though wondering how it had got out and what it was doing there without his permission, he still kept the cane pressed close to his spine, where it continued to wave gently from side to side, as though, like a dog's tail, it had a life of its own. Sunshine, it seemed to say, wouldn't last long if only Tommy could get at it.

Frequently, I carried a boys' paper in my satchel as a sort of promise of better things, and Downey watched me closely because he knew my weakness for glancing at it under my desk, as a man in mortal agony will glance at a crucifix. Once, he caught me with a paper called *The Scout* and held it up before the class with a roar of glee. "Ho! ho! ho!" he chortled. "Look who we have here! Look at our young scout! We'll soon knock the scouting out of him. . . . Hold out your hand, you little puppy!" I think he took more delight in catching us out than in beating us, because his stupidity was even greater than his brutality, if that was possible, and he seemed to regard all small boys as criminals with minds of extraordinary complexity and cunning, and greeted each new discovery of a plot with a sort of *Te Deum* of "Ho! ho! ho's," like a dictator who has just cracked a fresh liberal conspiracy.

The religious instruction never fell below the high standard of secular instruction set by Downey. We were prepared for our First Communion by a well-to-do old lady on Summerhill, who wore a black bonnet and cloak such as my grandmother wore on state occasions, and who was welcomed by Downey with the sugary amiability he otherwise reserved for his boss, the parish priest. She came to the school with a candle and a box of matches, stuck the candle on the desk before her and lit it. Then she put a half-crown beside the candle, and, when we had watched these fascinating preparations long enough, offered to give the half-crown to any small boy who would hold one finger— mind, only *one* finger!—in the candle flame for five minutes. Then, having studied us carefully, apparently waiting for offers, she cocked her head and said sharply: "And yet you'll risk an eternity of hell when you won't even put your finger in the candle flame for five minutes to earn half a crown!"

I think at any time I would cheerfully have risked

an eternity of hell sooner than spend a day in that school, and one of the few painful recollections I have of Mother is the morning she tried to pull me out from under the table to make me go to school, and I pulled the table along with me. On the other hand, when the impersonal brutality of doctor and dentist (there were no painless extractions for me) left me free, it was heaven to stand at the foot of Gardiner's Hill, sucking a sweet, and listen to the chant of the other victims roaring the multiplication table on the first three notes of the scale, as though at any moment they might burst into "Yankee Doodle," and catch a glimpse of Downey shooting past the front door, brandishing his cane. It enabled even a born Sir Galahad like myself to understand how, through all eternity, the blessed can contemplate the sufferings of the damned with no diminution of their own ecstasy. Anyone who was lucky enough to get out of that inferno, even for a day, had no time to spare for the sufferings of others.

Beside Downey, the assistants were all shadowy figures, like the kindly teacher we unkindly called "Tom Louse" who taught us Moore's lovely song "To Music," with its promise that when we grew up and life became harder, we would welcome such strains as these. In that atmosphere it made the future sound very unpromising. But one day an assistant came who made an immediate impression on my imagination. He was a small man with a lame leg who trailed slowly and painfully about the classrooms, though whenever he wanted to, he seemed to glide round on skates and had a violent temper that sent the blood rushing to his head. In spite of his affliction, he was like that, light and spare and clean. He had a small, round head, and a round face with a baby complexion on which a small, dark moustache and the shadow of a beard looked as inappropriate as they would have done on a small boy. His eyes were strange, because one eyebrow descended till it almost closed the eye, and the other mounted till it made the eye seem to expand. Afterwards, when I saw him do it with landscapes, I decided it was probably only a painter's trick of focusing a picture. His voice was the queerest part of him, because it had practically no modulation: each syllable emerged, harshly articulated and defined, with no perceptible variation of pitch, as though it were being cut off with a bacon slicer; and when he raised his voice, he raised his head as well, and pulled in his lower lip till the chin seemed to sag. That too someone explained to me later as a device for curing himself of a bad stammer, and it sounds probable enough, for though I did not realize it until later, the most striking thing about the Daniel Corkery of those years was his self-control.

One afternoon, at three o'clock, when we should have been going home, he kept us in, wrote a few words in a mysterious script on the top of the blackboard, and went on to give us our first lesson in what he called in his monosyllabic articulation "Eye Rish," a subject I had never heard of, but which seemed to consist of giving unfamiliar names to familiar objects. With my life-long weakness for interesting myself in matters that are no concern of mine, I noticed that he never referred once to the words on top of the blackboard. I waited politely until he was leaving, and then went up to him to ask what they meant. He smiled and said: "Waken your courage, Ireland!"—a most peculiar thing, as it seemed to me, for anyone to write on top of a blackboard, particularly when it didn't seem to be part of the lesson. He might, of course, have had a reason for not explaining it to the class, because the English were still in control, and neither they nor his other employers, the Roman Catholic Church, would have stood for much of that nonsense.

In singing class, instead of the Moore songs I loved, he taught us a song by someone called Walter Scott, which struck me as very dull indeed, and must have had a tune as uninteresting as the words, since a melomaniac like myself has forgotten it:

> *Breathes there a man with soul so dead*
> *Who never to himself has said*
> *"This is my own, my native land?"*

But I remember the angry passion with which he chopped off the syllables of the third line, flushing and tossing his small, dark head. I was too young to realize what he was doing—using the standard English texts to promote disaffection in the young, right under the nose of the old policeman-schoolmaster, Downey, and there must have even been moments when Downey suspected it, for though he was perceptibly more deferential to Corkery than to the other assistants, he sometimes stood and looked after him with a stunned air.

Still, wonders continued to occur. In the smaller classroom Corkery removed some charts of an informative kind and replaced them by two brightly coloured pictures that immediately engaged my roving attention. I had a passion for tracing and copying illustrations from magazines and books I had borrowed, which was the next best thing to owning the books myself, and it made me regard myself as something of an authority on art. I asked Corkery who had painted the pictures, and he smiled and said: "I did," as though he did not expect me to believe him. Really, they merely confirmed my favourable view of his abilities. They weren't *very* good pictures, not the sort that would

get into *The Boy's Own Paper,* but they showed promise. One was of a laneway in the Marsh with washing
strung from window to window across the dark lane,
and in the background a misty white tower that he
said was Shandon. It didn't look like Shandon, and I
told him so, but he said that this was the effect of the
light. The other picture was much stranger, for it
showed an old man facing the wall of a country cottage, playing his fiddle, and a small crowd standing
behind him. When I asked why the fiddler was looking
at the wall, Corkery explained that it was because he
was blind. If my memory of the picture is correct, he
had written beneath it twelve lines of verse in the peculiar script he used for Irish. I know that I learned
them, as I learned everything, by heart, and though
they bore out his explanation of why the fiddler did
not face the crowd, it still struck me as a tall story:

> *Look at me now!*
> *My face to the wall,*
> *Playing music*
> *To empty pockets.*

I took the poem home for my grandmother to in-
terpret. I had at last discovered some use for that extraordinary and irritating old woman, because it
turned out that Irish, not English, was her native language, as it was of several old people in the neighbourhood.

My grandmother didn't think much of the poem;
she said she knew better ones herself and wanted to
say them for me, but they were too hard, and she contented herself with teaching me my first sentence in
Irish—*A chailín óg, tabhair dhom póg, agus pósfaidh
mé thu* (Young girl, give me a kiss and I'll marry you).
No more than Downey's type of education did this

resemble anything I had read or heard of, but I found
it considerably more interesting.

Besides, as will become clear, I am a natural collaborationist; like Dolan's ass I go a bit of the road with
everybody, and I enjoyed having a hero among the
hereditary enemy—schoolmasters. I hung on to Corkery's coat-tails at lunch when he leaned against the
jamb of the front door, eating his sandwich; I borrowed Irish books from him that I could not understand, though this never hindered me from having a
crack at something, and sometimes I waited for him
after school to accompany him home as he butted his
way manfully up the cruel hill, sighing, his hat always
a little askew, one shoulder thrust forward like a swimmer, and the crippled foot trailing behind him. I imitated the old-fashioned grace with which he lifted his
hat and bowed slightly to any woman he recognized;
I imitated his extraordinary articulation so carefully
that to this day I can render it with what seems to me
complete fidelity, and for a time I even imitated his
limp. I never loved anyone without imitating him, and
having a quite satisfactory mother, I was not particularly attracted to women or girls, but in the absence of
a father who answered my needs, I developed fierce
passions for middle-aged men, and Corkery was my
first and greatest love. "Love" is a word that educa-
tionists dislike because it has so many unpleasant asso-
ciations, but it is a fact that in many children the
intellectual and emotional faculties are indissolubly
knit, and the one cannot develop without the other.
Any intellectual faculty I possessed was now developing like mad.

It developed so much that at Christmas Corkery—
out of his own pocket, I fancy—gave me a prize book
called *Kings and Vikings* by someone called Lorcan

O'Byrne, and this, being the only prize I ever received in any walk of life, has impressed itself on my memory. Of course, from Corkery's point of view, it was probably further subversive action, though I didn't realize this.

The headaches that had plagued me for a year were explained when a doctor sent me to have my eyes tested, and I had to wear black glasses and stop going to school for months. When I resumed, it was not at St. Patrick's but the North Monastery, run by the Christian Brothers—I cannot think why unless it meant that I should be out of Corkery's class and back in Downey's. Mother, I suspect, may have been influenced by her friendship with Mrs. Busteed, whom she met regularly at Mass, for her brilliant son, who had gone to the North Monastery, had had his picture in the paper and was now at the University, and it would never have occurred to Mother that what had worked for him would not work for me.

It was very inconvenient, because it was miles from home, and on rainy days I reached school drenched and cold. The road led past the military barrack on the brow of the hill and then down a dirt track called Fever Hospital Hill to the Brewery, before climbing again through slums to the top of another hill. But the view from Fever Hospital Hill was astonishing, and often delayed me when I was already late. The cathedral tower and Shandon steeple, all limestone and blue sandstone, soared off the edge of the opposite hill, and the hillside, terraced to the top with slums, stood so steep that I could see every lane in it, and when the light moved across it on a spring day, the whole hillside seemed to sway like a field of corn, and sometimes when there was no wind to stir the clouds, I could hear it murmuring to itself like a hive of bees.

I was happy enough for the first few months in a classroom where there was a statue of the Blessed Virgin (religious images were not allowed in the national schools), and when the best of the English compositions were shown along the partition in the classroom mine were often among them. But the monks had already made up their minds that I would never be a passer of examinations and never have my picture in the Cork *Examiner*, as John Busteed had. I was hurt when I was rejected from the singing class because of my defective ear because I knew perfectly well that my ear was not defective. Overenthusiastic, perhaps—it still is, since my temperament makes me rush at things I like without paying too much attention to intervals and time—but not defective. And yet I had to sit there, listening to songs I loved without being allowed to join in them. It was very hard.

However, I was busy in other fields. The First World War had broken out; Father was called up, leaving comparative peace in the home, though, to make up for that, my grandfather had died and my grandmother had come to live with us. Inflamed with emotion by the supposed atrocities of the Germans against the Belgians, I had engaged in beating them myself in my own small way. On the kitchen wall I had pinned a map of the Western Front into which I stuck flags to show the position of the two armies, and I conducted brilliant campaigns of my own that beat the Germans to their knees in twenty-four hours. Father was also conducting a campaign, the details of which eluded me till later, but it was much more practical than mine. He loved pensions, and as there was no chance of a service pension out of the War, he was quietly building up a case history of rheumatic pains that would get him a disability pension when the War came to an end. Not a very large pension; you can't do much with occasional rheumatism, and anything more might have caused him to be sent home, but every little helps.

Father, I am certain, really enjoyed the War in the way that a middle-aged man enjoys a second marriage—as a renewal of youth. Though he liked his brief and dangerous reunions with his family, he was an old soldier among a whole army of young ones; he could make himself comfortable where they died of misery, and he enjoyed his opportunities for wangling, and never came home without his pockets and kit-bag filled with bits of equipment that would all come in useful if he kept them for seven years. But Mother and I had never been happier. For the first time since I knew her, she had a regular allowance, and I had regular pocket money which I divided up between boys' weeklies and illustrated papers that dealt with the story of the War. I was interested in the War, not only because Father was engaged in it, but because there were several Belgian kids in my class at school who had been driven from their homes by the Germans. They lived in the big Montenotte house of the Countess Murphy. The Countess had been one of my big disappointments. Her companion was another of the orphans, called Kate Gaynor, but Kate's family had apparently been well-to-do, and she and her sister had gone to the Orphanage as paying pupils. They were brought up a little apart from the other orphans and allowed to continue their piano lessons. Kate was a stiff, pompous woman with a cutting tongue, and she and Mother disagreed—in so far as Mother disagreed with anybody—about the Orphanage. Nothing would ever have induced Mother to say a word against it, but Kate said bitterly that if she had her way all the orphanages in the world would be torn to the ground because they "robbed a child of natural affections." What she meant by that, I realized later, was that in middle age it left her nobody to love but an aging, cranky woman.

The Countess (the title was a Papal one, for the Count, who, I think, was a brewer, had written a defence of Catholicism that was always on view on the drawing-room table) had been very impressed by my good manners and piety, and promised to provide for my education as a priest. For a little while this made Mother and myself almost insane with happiness. But one Christmas either the Countess or Kate gave me a painting book and a box of paints, and, never having had paints to play with before, I had a beautiful time with them. When next Kate visited us and inspected the painting book, she asked in a cold, disgusted voice where I had seen green cows. Mother and I were equally mortified at my lack of observation, and when the Countess died, having failed to provide for my education as a priest, I was left with the guilty feeling that I had forever forfeited my hope of advancement by failing to notice that cows were not green.

And now the Countess was dead, and the beautiful house on Montenotte was a hostel for Belgian refugees, and whenever we knocked on her door Kate called out wearily *"Entrez."* She found the refugees disgusting, but I was devoted to them, first because they had been driven from their homes by the beastly Germans like the Holy Family by Herod, and second, because they spoke a different language. In the North Monastery we said our prayers in Irish, a language I had begun to lose interest in because it was obviously useless in the modern world. The Belgians said theirs in Flemish, and I was not happy till I could do the same. For some time after that I never used any other language for my night and morning prayers. The monks were wrong in thinking me a complete fool: I was really a serious student, but it was always of something that could be of no earthly use to me; which is probably why they summoned Mother to the school and explained to her that I would never be able to pass the regular Intermediate examinations, and put me into the Trades School, where I could pick up something more suitable to my station in life than Flemish. It was a blow to both of us, because, though it closed the doors of the University on me, it did not open the door of the trades. Entry to these was regulated by their own unions.

In the Trades School I didn't pick up anything at all, useful or otherwise, though I liked Murray, the tall, gloomy, sardonic monk who taught us in an atmosphere of complete hopelessness, as though he knew he had been given the job only because he could not teach and we had been sent to him only because we could not learn. I still read English school stories, and modelled myself entirely on the characters in them, and this continued to get me into trouble because neither Murray nor my classmates had read them, nor indeed anything else that I could ever discover, and continued to treat me as though I were slightly insane. It culminated in a scene when myself and another quiet boy were attacked on our way home from school by a real little fighter. Cowardice was no name for my normal attitude to violence; I slunk home through the streets like one of those poor mongrels that Minnie Connolly sympathized so much with, who flitted from

pavement to pavement in an effort to avoid their tor-
mentors, but when I was roused, I had my father's
murderous temper, and on this occasion at least, I
managed to damage the other boy's mouth and leave
him weeping.

I can prove that I was alone in reading English
school stories because next morning he complained to
Murray—a thing nobody in an English school story
would do—and when Murray questioned me I told the
truth and took the blame, which was an offence in itself, since Irish schoolteachers tend to regard truthful-
ness as Irish farmers regard the old-fashioned Quaker
refusal to haggle—as something unneighbourly. Murray, with his morbid, dyspeptic humour, thought it a
neat idea to give my opponent his strap and order him
to punish us himself. He did this with my companion,
and the class, which was almost as mature as Murray,
thought it an excellent joke, but when it came to my
turn I told Murray that if he came near me I would
knock him down. Murray—not an unkind man—became a bright brick red and turned nasty, but I was
fighting mad and stood my ground. Of course, I paid
dear for the pleasure of spoiling his idea of a good
joke, but it was one of the few occasions when I had
no regrets for having made a fool of myself.

Then my grandmother died. In the early hours of
the morning my uncle went for the priest and came in
with him looking very pale. As they passed a forge,
Father Tierney had said: "Get off the foot-path and let
the ghosts go by," which admittedly was enough to
make any man go pale. In the manner of the old country people, my grandmother was well prepared for
death. For as long as I remembered her, she had been
giving instructions for her funeral, and Father, the
tease of the family, had told her he couldn't afford to

take her back to her own people, at which Grandmother had told him she would haunt him. In a drawer she had the two bits of blessed candle that were to be lit over her when she died, and her shroud, which she took out regularly to air on the line. She was ill for a week or two and lay upstairs, saying her beads and reciting poetry in Irish. The day before she died she shouted for a mirror, and Mother told her she should be thinking of God, but the old woman only shouted louder. When Mother brought the mirror upstairs, Grandmother studied herself for a few moments in stupefaction and muttered: "Jesus Christ, there's a face!" before turning to the wall. She had not wanted to rejoin her dead husband, looking like that.

Afterwards we had perfect peace in the house till Father returned from the Army. Mother scrubbed out the bedroom and coloured it a warm pink; she sewed pretty curtains for the attic window and dolled up an old orange-box as a bookcase for me. My books didn't amount to much, but I cheated quite a bit. There was, for instance, the sixpenny Shakespeare which I tore up and rebound as individual plays. There were also tracts you could buy for a penny in the church that made quite impressive titles. My files of boys' weeklies and war papers were ranged along the floor under the attic window. Mother had taught me to make rough binding cases for them, and of course I had a neat catalogue, modelled on the catalogue of the public library, for I was nothing if not orderly, and I never admired anything without trying to imitate it. After some friends of Mother's had taken us to a matinee of *Carmen*, I began another catalogue of operas I had heard, but this never amounted to much. The invaluable boys' weeklies described how to do everything, and being in most ways a very ordinary boy, according to my lights and equipment I did it, from making a model aeroplane (that wouldn't fly) to a telephone (that wouldn't talk), though, when I got down to making gunpowder I did blow the eyebrows and eyelashes off the unfortunate boy who was with me. I even made a model theatre out of an old boot-box with a proscenium arch and a selection of back-drops all painted by myself that represented backgrounds in Spain, Italy, and other operatic countries; characters traced from illustrations in library books which I coloured and mounted on sticks; and an elaborate lighting system of Christmas-tree candles with coloured slides of greased paper that could be made to produce the effect of moonlight, dawn, storm, and every other romantic aspect of nature. I played with this for hours in the dark hallway, singing arias, duets, and trios that I made up as I went along.

The boys' weeklies were now the only form of education I had because I had given up school. There must have been some illness to account for this, but I am quite sure that if there was I extracted the last ounce of agony and weakness from it, because I loathed the Trades School and took advantage of every excuse to avoid attending it. Father's absence at the War was a mixed blessing, because it left Mother unprotected against me, and I was every bit as ruthless as he was.

13

IN APRIL 1916 a handful of Irishmen took over
the city of Dublin and were finally surrounded and overwhelmed by British troops with artillery. The daily papers showed Dublin as they showed
Belgian cities destroyed by the Germans, as smoking
ruins inhabited by men with rifles and machine guns.
At first my only reaction was horror that Irishmen
could commit such a crime against England. I was
sure that phase had ended with the Boer War in which
Father had fought, because one of his favourite songs
said so:

> *You used to call us traitors because*
> *of agitators,*
> *But you can't call us traitors now.*

But the English were calling us traitors again, and they seemed to be right. It was a difficult situation for a boy of twelve with no spiritual homeland but that of the English public schools, and no real friends but those imaginary friends he knew there. I had defended their code of honour with nothing to support me but faith, and now, even if the miracle happened and Big Tim Fahy returned from Chicago with bags of money and sent me to school in England, I should be looked on with distrust—almost, God help me, as if I were a German who said *Donner und Blitzen,* which was what all Germans said.

The English shot the first batch of Irish leaders, and this was a worse shock, for the newspapers said— the pro-British ones with a sneer—that several of them had been poets, and I was in favour of poets. One of them, Patrick Pearse, on the night before his execution had written some poems, one of them to his mother —which showed him a man of nice feeling—and another, which contained lines I still remember:

The beauty of this world hath made me sad—
This beauty that will pass.
Sometimes my heart hath shaken with great joy
To see a leaping squirrel in a tree,
Or a red ladybird upon a stalk . . .

What made it worse was that most of his poetry had been written in Irish, the language I had abandoned in favour of Flemish. And Corkery, who had introduced me to Irish, I had not seen for years. But I still had an old primer that had been thrown into a corner, and I started trying to re-learn all that I had forgotten. A revolution had begun in Ireland, but it was nothing to the revolution that had begun in me. It is only in the imagination that the great tragedies take place, and I had only my imagination to live in. I enjoyed English school stories as much as ever, but already I was developing a bad conscience about them. The heroes of those stories, the Invisible Presences, I knew, must look on me as a traitor. They reminded me of how they had taken me in and made me one of themselves, and I had to reply that if I was different, it was because of what they and theirs had done to make me so. For months I read almost nothing but Irish history and the result was horrifying. I wrote my first essay, which listed all the atrocities I could discover that had been committed by the English in the previous hundred years or so, but it had no more effect than the deceived husband's listing of his wife's infidelities has on his need for her. My heart still cried out for the Invisible Presences.

In the early mornings Mother and I went into town to the Franciscan or Augustinian church where Mass was said for the dead rebels, and on the way back we bought picture postcards of them. One afternoon when we were walking in the country we met Corkery, and I asked him how I could take up Irish again. After that I went on Saturday afternoons to the children's class at the Gaelic League hall in Queen Street. The Irish we spoke was of less importance to me than the folk songs we learned, and these than the kilt that one of the boys wore. I felt my own position keenly. Not only was I suspect to the Invisible Presences; with a father and uncle in the British Army I was suspect to loyal children as well. But no one could suspect the loyalty of a boy who wore a kilt, and I persecuted my mother till she made one for me. She did not find it easy, as kilts were not worn in her young days.

Somewhere or other I had picked up Eleanor

Hull's *Cuchulain,* a re-telling of the Ulster sagas for
children, and that became a new ideal. Nobody in any
English school story I had read had done things as remarkable as that child had done by the age of seven.
But for me, even his deeds were small compared with
what he said when he actually was seven and some
druid prophesied a short life for him. "Little I care
though I were to live but a day and a night if only my
fame and adventures lived after me." No one had ever
better expressed my own view of life.

Having exhausted most of the books in the children's department of the library, I had discovered the
adult one, and, by using a ticket I had got for Mother,
I could borrow a school story from upstairs and a book
on history downstairs. It took real courage to face the
adult library of those days. There was a card catalog
and a long counter surmounted by a primitive device
known as an Indicator—a huge glass case where all
the book numbers were shown in blue (which meant
they were available) or red (which meant they were
not). If you were a scholarly person and could deduce
from the author and title whether a book was readable
or not, it didn't matter perhaps, but if, like me, you
knew nothing about books, you might often walk back
the two miles home in rage and disgust with something
you couldn't even read. Education was very hard.

One of the grown-up books I borrowed was O'Curry's *Manuscript Materials,* which contained a lot about
Cu Chulainn. No more than O'Curry himself was I put
off by the fact that this was in a form of Irish I didn't
know, ranging from the eighth to the twelfth century
(I never allowed myself to be deflected by details);
and, casting myself in the part of a mediaeval scribe, I
copied it out with coloured initials imitated from the
Book of Kells.

157

But though I knew as little about the hero of a modern English public-school story as I did about the hero of a primitive saga, imitating the one turned out to be child's play compared with imitating the other, and I nearly ruptured myself trying to perform the least of the feats Cu Chulainn had performed when he was barely half my age. It seemed I had wasted my time practising with a bow, for the Irish had no use for it, and I had to begin all over again with a slingshot; but though I practised hard, I never came within measurable distance of killing someone in a crowd half a mile away. It was difficult enough to hit a gate post at twenty yards, and even then my heart was in my mouth for fear I should break a window and have the police after me.

Most of my endeavours were wasted on a single episode in Cu Chulainn's infancy. He left home when he was little more than a toddler, hurling his toy spear before him, pucking his hurling ball after that, throwing his hurling stick after the ball, and then catching all three before they alighted. No one who has not tried that simple feat can imagine how difficult it is. There was more sense in the story of how he killed the great watch-dog by throwing the hurling ball down its gullet and then beating it over the head with his hurley, and I practised that, too, beginning with very small dogs; but, knowing my character much better than I did, they decided I only wanted to play with them, and ran away with the ball. When they finally let me catch up on them and grinned at me with the ball between their teeth, I could no more hit them with the hurley than I could do anything else that Cu Chulainn had done. I was crazy about dogs and cats. I saw clearly that the Irish race had gone to hell since saga

158

times, and that this was what had enabled the English to do what they liked with us.

Queer treasures I clutched to my chest, coming over Parnell Bridge in the evening on my way from the Public Library. Once it was a collection of Irish folk music, and I proudly copied the O'Donovan clan march in staff notation, hoping to find someone who would sing it to me. Father had earlier discovered the O'Donovan coat of arms, and I had discovered that there was a village called Castle Donovan in West Cork. The family was obviously something. Sometimes I took out in Mother's name an art book or a novel by Canon Sheehan, who was parish priest of a County Cork town, and had a most unclerical passion for novel writing. He had been greatly praised by a Russian writer called Tolstoy, and later I learned that his clerical enemies had sent one of his novels to Rome in the hope of having it condemned for heresy, but the Papal authorities, mistaking the purpose of the submission, gave Sheehan a D.D. instead. He shared with the authors of the boys' weeklies a weakness for foreign languages, and printed lengthy extracts from Goethe in the original, and ever since I have been torn between two attitudes to this practice. With one half of my mind I regard it as detestable snobbery, but with the other I think it the only sensible way of influencing young people like myself. If the original monkey had not despised monkeys he would never have invented clothes, and I should not have bothered to learn Goethe's *Symbolen* by heart. Never having anyone to teach me, I learned only by pretending to know. I played at reading foreign languages and tenth-century Irish, at being a priest and saying Mass, at singing from staff notation and copying out pieces of music when I didn't know one note from another, at being a painter and a theatrical producer. It is not a form of education I would recommend to anyone, nor should I ever get a degree in French, German, Latin, music, or even Middle Irish, but I still catch myself out at it, playing at scholarship and correcting the experts, and sometimes a little streak of lunatic vanity that runs through it all suggests that I may be right and everybody else wrong.

Mother must have been astonished at becoming a borrower of art books containing pictures of naked gods and goddesses in queer positions, and I had great difficulty in persuading the stupid girls in the Carnegie Library who tried to stop me taking them out that they were Mother's favourite reading, but I knew I should never become a great painter unless I could copy Bronzino and Tintoretto and learn all about the rules of perspective and chiaroscuro, and there is a sort of irresistible force behind a small spectacled boy with an aim in life. At the same time I was astonished at the modesty of the Renaissance artists who painted women different from men, and I still remember the stunned look on Mother's face when I commented on it to her. "Difference of sex I never knew more than the guardian angels do," but I was broad-minded, and I realized that, for the common run of people, such frankness might not do.

I had my greatest shock in that same year, 1916, when, passing by O'Keeffe's bookshop in Great George's Street one evening, I saw a book called *A Munster Twilight* of which the author was someone named Daniel Corkery. It seemed altogether too much of a coincidence to presume that the author could be my old teacher, and even if I had had a shilling (the price of the book) I dared not have risked it on such a slender possibility. But it stuck in my mind, and when next I waylaid Corkery, he admitted that he was the author. I was instantly struck with awe—not only at the man's ability, but at my own shrewdness in having discovered him before anyone else had done so. Cu Chulainn might have been able to smash bronze chariots with his bare fists and capture whole flocks of birds alive with a single throw of his slingshot—a most difficult feat, as I had discovered by experiment—but there was no evidence of his ever having had an eye for talent.

I borrowed the book from the Public Library and one day when Mother was at work I sat on a warm rock at the foot of the square and read steadily through it without understanding a word. It was not as good as the *Gem* or the *Magnet*, but Corkery certainly had talent. I was interested principally in what it said about me, but, beyond referring to some ancient West Cork poet called Owen More O'Donovan, Corkery seemed to be keeping our acquaintance dark.

And that settled the hash of the English boys' weeklies. I did not know their authors as I knew Corkery, and henceforth their creations would be less real to me than his, little as I might understand them. And one day I woke to find the Invisible Presences of my childhood departing with a wave of the hand as they passed forever from sight. Not angrily, nor even reproachfully, but sadly, as good friends part, and even when I grew up, and had other presences to think of, I continued to remember them for what they had been —a child's vision of a world complete and glorified.

14

BY THE TIME I was fourteen it was clear that
education was something I would never be
able to afford. Not that I had any intention of giving
it up even then. I was just looking for a job that
would enable me to buy the books from which I could
pick up the education myself. So, with the rest of the
unemployed, I went to the newsroom of the Carnegie
Library where on wet days the steam heating warmed
the perished bodies in the broken boots and made the
dirty rags steam and smell. I read carefully through the
advertisements and applied for every job that demanded "a smart boy," but what I really hoped for was
to find a new issue of the *Times Literary Supplement,*
The Spectator, The New Statesman, or *The Studio* free,
so that I could read articles about books and pictures

I would never see, but as often as not some hungry old man would have toppled asleep over it, and I was cheated. The real out-of-works always favoured the high-class magazines at which they were unlikely to be disturbed, though occasionally some cranky ratepayer would rouse the Lancashire librarian in his rubber-soled shoes, and the out-of-work would be shaken awake and sent to take his rest elsewhere. Then, divided between the claims of pity and justice, I went out myself and wandered aimlessly round town till hunger or darkness or rain sent me home.

"A smart boy's" was the job I needed, because, when it became clear that I would never be a priest, Mother's only ambition was for me to become a clerk —someone who would wear a white collar and be called "Mister." Knowing no better myself, but always willing—up to a point—always visiting the Carnegie Library or the advertisement board in front of the Cork *Examiner* office, and answering advertisements for a smart boy, I went to the Technical School and the School of Commerce at night to learn whatever I could learn there in the way of arithmetic, book-keeping and short-hand typewriting. Of book-keeping, all I ever could remember was a saying quoted approvingly on the first page of our textbook—written, of course, by the headmaster himself—which ran: "In business, there is no such thing as an out-and-out free gift"; and of typewriting, a fascinating example of punctuation that began: "The splendour falls on castle walls," which I promptly got by heart. Perhaps they stuck so firmly in my mind because they represented the two irreconcilables that I was being asked to reconcile in myself.

In the pursuit of what I regarded as serious education, I also worked hard at a Self-Educator I had picked up, God knows where. From Canon Sheehan's novels I had deduced that German was the real language of culture and that the greatest of cultured persons was Goethe, so I read right through Goethe in English and studied German out of the Self-Educator so as to be able to read him in the original. I was impressed by the fact that one of the pretty songs Mother had taught me as a child—"Three Students Went Merrily over the Rhine"—turned up in a German anthology as a real poem by a real German poet, so I learned the German words and sang them instead. I also made a valiant attempt to learn Greek, which struck me as a very important cultural medium indeed, being much more difficult than Latin, but as I had never learned the rudiments of grammar in any language I never got far with Greek.

I got my first job through my confessor, a gentle old priest who regarded me as a very saintly boy, and regularly asked me to pray for his intention. If innocence and sanctity are related, he was probably not so far wrong about me because once I confessed to "bad thoughts," meaning, I suppose, murdering my grandmother, but Father O'Regan interpreted it differently, and there ensued an agonizing few minutes in which he asked me questions I didn't understand, and I gave him answers that he didn't understand, and I suspect that when I left the confession box, the poor man was as shaken as I was.

The job was in a pious wholesale drapery business where every member of the staff had apparently been recommended by his confessor, and I hated my immediate boss, a small, smug, greasy little shopman with a waxed black moustache who tried hard to teach me that whenever he called "O'Donovan!" I was instantly to drop whatever I was doing and rush to him, crying smartly "Yessir!" I never minded dropping what I was

doing, which was usually folding shirts as if I were laying out a corpse—the two arms neatly across the breast
—and I had no objection to calling anybody "Sir," but
it was several seconds before my armour of day-dreaming was penetrated by a voice from outside and "The
splendour falls on castle walls" gave place to the stern
beauty of "In business, there is no such thing as an out-
and-out free gift," and it was several seconds more before I realized that it was the voice to which I must
reply "Yessir!" so at the end of a fortnight I stopped folding shirts and saying "Yessir!" and went home to put
in some more work at Greek. Then I tried a spell in a
chemist's shop that was looking for a smart boy, but I
soon discovered that I was only needed to deliver messages and that no amount of smartness would ever
make a chemist of me. I still have a vivid recollection
of the end of this job. I was still a small boy, and I was
looking up at a tall counter, and leaning on the counter
and looking down at me through his glasses was a tall,
thin Dublinman, just back from a visit to the pub next
door. He was telling me in a thick Dublin accent that I
had no notion of the sort of people I was working for,
and begging me earnestly, for Christ's sweet sake and
my own good, to get to hell out of it, quick. I got to hell
out of it quick all right.

There was an even briefer spell at a job printer's,
because while he was showing me the ropes, the printer
asked was I any good at spelling, and I replied airily:
"Oh, that's my forte!" Now, that was exactly the sort of
language we used on the heights, and I wasn't conscious of doing anything wrong in using it, but that
evening the man who had recommended me to the
printer met me and repeated the story of my reply with
a great deal of laughter, and I realized that, as usual,
I had made a fool of myself. It was part of the abnor-

mal sensitiveness induced by day-dreaming, and I was so mortified that I never went back. I was sorry for that, because I really was quite good at spelling, and I still feel I should have made an excellent compositor.

Instead, this only became an additional weight in the load of guilt I always carried. It seemed that I could never persevere with anything, school or work, and just as I had always been impressed by the view of other small boys that I was mad, I was beginning to be impressed by their parents' view that I was a good-for-nothing who would never be anything but a burden on his father and mother. God knows, Father had impressed it on me often enough.

I went to the railway as a messenger boy because I despaired of ever becoming anything better, and besides, though the hours—eight to seven—were hard, the pay—a pound a week—was excellent, and with money like that coming in I could buy a lot of books and get a lot of education. It was with real confidence that at last the future had something in store for me that I left the house one morning at half-past seven and went down Summerhill and the tunnel steps to go to the Goods Office on the quay. Upstairs in the long office where the invoice clerks worked under the eye of the Chief Clerk, I met the other junior tracers, Sheehy, Cremin, and Clery, and the two senior tracers. Our job was to assist the invoice and claims clerks, bringing in dockets from the storage shed and enquiring in the storage shed for missing goods—hence our title.

All transport companies have colossal claims for missing goods, many of which are not really missing at all but lying about forgotten. Whisky and tobacco were easy to trace because they had to be loaded into sealed wagons before some old railway policeman who recorded them and the number of the wagon in his little red book. But no one took much responsibility for other articles, and it depended on the memory of the checkers whether or not you could discover what had happened to them. An efficient, friendly checker like Bob St. Leger of the Dublin Bay or Leahy of the Fermoy Bay could often remember a particular consignment, and, if he were in good humour, could fish it out from the corner where it had lain for weeks, covered by a heap of fresh merchandise. This was a triumph, and you marked your memorandum or wire with some code word like "Stag," meaning that the thing was at last on its way. But, more often, nobody remembered anything at all, and then you wrote something else, like "Bison," which meant "Certainly forwarded please say if since received," to which Goold's Cross or Farranfore retorted "Moose," meaning that it wasn't, and then you had to go to the storage shed and search through scores of tall dusty wire files to discover the original docket and the name of the checker or porter who had signed the receipt for it.

It didn't take me long to realize that this was only going to be another version of school, a place where I would be always useless, frightened, or hurt. The other messengers were railwaymen's sons and understood the work as though they had been born to it. Sheehy was thin, with high cheekbones and an impudent smile; Cremin was round-faced, cherry-cheeked, and complacent, and shot about the office and the store almost without raising his feet. Young Sheehy sneered at me all the time, but young Cremin only sneered at me part of the time because he was usually so busy with his own jobs that he hadn't time for anyone else's, but a couple of times when I found myself with some job I could not do, he looked at me for a while with pity and contempt and then took it from me and did it himself. "See?" he would crow. "Dead easy!" Cremin was really what the advertisements meant when they asked for a smart boy. Years later I found myself in the same hut in an internment camp with him, and though our positions had changed somewhat by that time, and I was a teacher, he was still the same smart boy, mixing with nobody in particular though amiable with everybody, briskly hammering rings out of shilling pieces or weaving macramé handbags—a cheerful, noisy, little universe of self-satisfaction. Yet the moment I fell ill, he nursed me with the same amused exasperation with which he had found dockets for me on the railway, cluck-clucking with an amused smile at my inability to do anything for myself.

My boss was obviously a man who had also at one time been a smart boy and owed his promotion to it. He had a neat, swift hand, and I imitated his elegant signature as I imitated Corkery's articulation, in a hopeless attempt at becoming a smart boy myself. He had a fat, pale face, a button of a nose with a pince-nez attached that was for ever dropping off and being retrieved just in time; he dressed excellently and swept through the office and the storage shed with an air of efficiency that must long since have secured his promotion to the job of stationmaster in Borrisokane or Goold's Cross. I fancy he was really clever and not unkind, but as the days went by he became more and more infuriated by my slowness and stupidity; and, having readjusted his pince-nez sternly, he would shout abuse at me till the whole office was listening and the other messengers sniggering, and I slunk away, stupider than ever, muttering aspirations to the Sacred Heart and the Blessed Virgin to assist me in whatever impossible task I was being asked to perform. It was one of the

senior tracers who, in mockery of my love of Irish and
the gilt ring I wore in my coat, nicknamed me "The
Native," but it was the boss who perpetuated it. It was
characteristic of Ireland at the time that the mere fact
that you spoke Irish could make you be regarded as a
freak.

The other clerk for whom I had to do odd jobs
was a very different type. He was small, fair-haired,
red-cheeked, and untidy, and drifted about the office
with his hands in his trousers pockets, wearing an in-
credible expression of sweetness and wonder as though
he were imitating some saint and martyr he had heard
of in church. Either he would put his arm about my
waist and draw me close to him, calling me "Child,"
and beg me in a low, quavering voice to assist him—
that is if I could spare him a couple of minutes—or
else he would call "Boy!" in a faraway tone, and look at
me as though wondering who I was, and rush after me,
tearing papers from my hand and scolding and nagging
till my nerves were on edge. Then he would sit on his
high stool, his fat hands clasped between his thighs,
staring incredulously after me.

Not that I didn't do my best. God knows I did. One
of my jobs was to answer the telephone, and I did it
with such intensity that I could never hear a word
the other person said, and so developed a hatred of
telephones that has lasted to this day. If there is anything unnaturally stupid or compromising a man can
say, I am always guaranteed to say it on the telephone.
Sometimes, when I was alone in the Goods Office I
listened miserably to some message, too ashamed to admit that I hadn't understood it. Sometimes I summoned
up courage and said that I couldn't hear, and then the
person at the other end always got furious—a fatal
thing to do with me as it drives me completely dis-

tracted—and asked if there was no one on the Great Southern and Western Railway who was not stone deaf. Having it put to me like that, I could only reply that there was but he was out at lunch. And whatever stupid thing I said always got back to the boss.

The trouble was that I could not believe in the telephone or the messages that came by it. I could not believe that the missing goods I was supposed to trace had ever existed, or if they had, that their loss meant anything to anybody. Being a naturally kind-hearted boy, if I had believed it I would have found them whatever it cost me. All I could believe in was words, and I clung to them frantically. I would read some word like "unsophisticated" and at once I would want to know what the Irish equivalent was. In those days I didn't even ask to be a writer; a much simpler form of transmutation would have satisfied me. All I wanted was to translate, to feel the unfamiliar become familiar, the familiar take on all the mystery of some dark foreign face I had just glimpsed on the quays.

I hated the storeroom where the dockets were kept, and when I worked there with Sheehy, Cremin, or Clery, I realized that they found six dockets in the time it took me to find one. I had poor sight, and often failed to see a docket properly, particularly as it was usually written in the semi-literate scrawl of carters or porters; and even when I should have seen it, my mind was on something else, and when it was not, it was harassed by panic, shyness, and ignorance. Bad as the storage shed was, noisy, evil-smelling, and dark except where it was pitted with pale electric lights, I preferred it to the office because a couple of the men were kind and did not lose their tempers with me. But even here I was at a disadvantage. Sheehy and Cremin, being railwaymen's sons, were protected by their fathers' presence from anything worse than good-natured ragging, but I was anybody's butt, and was for ever being pawed by two of the men. One, a foul-mouthed old ruffian with streaming white hair, didn't seem to mind when I edged away from him, but the other—a younger man with a thin, handsome, cruel face—resented it and hated me. I was always being mystified by the abrupt changes in his manner, for at one moment he would be smooth-spoken, dignified, and considerate, and at the next his delicate complexion would grow brilliant red, and in a low, monotonous voice he would spew out abuse and filth at me, and I never could see why. It didn't even need my timid attempts to dodge his brutal goosing and pawing; anything did it, a word, or a tone of voice, or simply nothing at all that I could observe. But how little there was that I could observe!

There was, for instance, the matter of "1 Bale Foreskins" which appeared on a docket and was invoiced to Kingsbridge by some bored young invoice clerk. Kingsbridge, equally full of bored young men, solemnly replied, reporting that the bale of foreskins had not been received and asking that it should be traced. It was my duty to trace it, and I did so with my usual earnestness, enquiring of every checker and porter in the neighbourhood of the Dublin bay if perhaps a bale of foreskins might not still be lying round somewhere. They listened to me with great attention and asked what I thought it looked like, and I explained that I didn't know, but that it was probably like any other bale of pelts. They assured me that there were no pelts lying round anywhere, and when I had looked for myself I marked the memorandum "Stag" or "Falcon" or whatever the code word was. But then the wires began to fly, and I had to visit the storage shed

again to make another search and find the docket in
the files. To me the docket looked like any other docket,
though later I realized that the names of consignor and
consignee would have revealed to any smart boy that
it was all a practical joke. But, in fact, so far as I was
concerned the docket was not more unreal than any
other docket, and the bale of foreskins than any other
bale, and these than the pawing of the workmen. They
were all just a vast phantasmagoria which I had to pretend to believe in to draw my weekly pay, but I never
did believe in it, and when I left the building at seven
o'clock it faded like clouds in the sky. At the same time
I envied people who did believe in it, like young
Cremin, and I pitied myself when I saw him, storming
through the shed, from one lamp-lit bay to the next, his
bundle of documents in his hand, exchanging noisy
greetings with the porters, dodging checkers who tried
to grab him, and yelling back laughing insults at them
—at home with everybody but most of all with himself.
In that whole huge organization there wasn't a soul
with whom I felt at home, and so I had no self to be at
home with; the only self I knew being then in wait for
me until seven o'clock in the passenger station at the
other side of the tracks, rather as I waited for Father
outside a public house.

There was one checker I liked, and though he always nodded gravely to me and was helpful on the very
few occasions when I needed his help, he never became
involved with me. I think he realized with the force of
revelation that I didn't believe in dockets and bales of
pelts, and was doomed to trouble and that this trouble
would fall on anyone who had anything to do with me.
He shuffled through the storage shed with his head
buried in his shoulders and a little to one side as though
he hoped no one would notice him, his short-sighted

blue eyes narrowed into slits. His secret was that he didn't believe in these things either. At the same time the feeling of his own peril gave him a certain guilty feeling of responsibility to me because I was clearly so much more imperilled than he was, and occasionally he stopped to talk to me and shuffled inch by inch out of the way into some corner where we could not be observed. Then, looking furtively over a bale of goods to make sure that no one was listening, he would tell me in a whisper that the country was priest-ridden. I didn't know what he meant by that, but I knew he meant that I had his sympathy. I was for the lions, and family conditions compelled him to burn a pinch of incense now and again, but he and I both knew there was no such God as Jupiter. One day, with a display of caution that would have done credit to an international conspirator, he pulled me aside, opened his blue jacket with the silver buttons, and took out a book which he thrust on me.

"Read that, boy," he whispered. "That'll show you what the country is really like."

The book was *Waiting* by Gerald O'Donovan, an interesting novelist now almost forgotten. He was a priest in Loughrea who had been carried away by the Catholic liberal movement and the Irish national movement. Later, in disgust with his bishop, he became an army chaplain, married, and wrote a number of novels that have authenticity without charm. I read the book with great care, though a boy who didn't know what a foreskin was had little chance of understanding what the country was like. Yet I remember that particular checker for the breath of fresh air he brought for a moment into my life, with its guarantee that the reality of dockets and invoices, smart boys and foul-mouthed workers, was not quite as real as it seemed.

There was one further small reference to the world I really believed in in a kilted man who appeared one day at the office counter, apparently about some missing goods but who refused to speak English. Cremin came back from the counter, looking red, and reported to my boss. Obviously, this was a very tasteless joke, and the boss shot out, adjusting his pince-nez with the air of a man who never stood any nonsense. But it was no joke. French the visitor would speak if he was compelled, but Irish was the language of his choice, and nobody in the office except myself spoke a word of French or Irish. Nobody outside my boss and the other tracers even bothered to jeer me about my weakness for Irish, though one clerk, a small prissy man with pince-nez, did once sniff at me and ask me what literature we had in Irish to compare with Shakespeare. For a few minutes there was consternation as the clerks discussed the irruption. "All right, Native," the boss said at last with the air of a man setting a thief to catch a thief. "You'd better see what he wants."

Of course, the stranger turned out to be an Englishman, the son of an Anglican bishop, who was enjoying the embarrassment he was causing in an Irish railway station by speaking Irish when the only person who could answer him was a messenger boy. And, indeed, the matter didn't end there, because the Englishman had to put in his claim, and put it in in Irish, which I had to translate into English, and the clerks decided to get even with him by making me also translate the official reply into Irish. Of course, he was a sport and I was a fool, but the little incident was a slight indication of a revolution that was already taking place without the smart boys even being aware of it.

It was also an indication of the extraordinary double life I was leading, a life so divided against itself that it comes back to me now as a hallucination rather than as a memory. Usually, there is some connection between the real and imaginary worlds, some acquaintance in whom the two temporarily merge, but when I left the railway I did not leave a friend behind me and never so much as enquired what had happened to any of the decent people I knew there. One life I led in English—a life of drudgery and humiliation; the other in Irish or whatever scraps of foreign languages I had managed to pick up without benefit of grammar, and which any sensible man would describe as day-dreaming, though day-dreaming is a coarse and unrealistic word that might be applied by sensible men to the beliefs of the early Christians. That was the real significance of my passion for languages: they belonged entirely to the world of my imagination, and even today, when some figure of fantasy enters my dreams, he or she is always liable to break into copious and inaccurate French—the imagination seems to have no particular use for grammar. Irish was merely the most convenient of these escape routes into dreams, and that was why, on Saturday nights, with a German book from the Carnegie Library under my arm, I attended lectures in the Gaelic League hall in Queen Street, or stood admiringly in a corner listening to my seniors discussing in Irish profound questions such as "Is Shakespeare national?" and "Is dancing immoral?" or perhaps "Is dancing national?" and "Is Shakespeare immoral?" I still had no education, except such as fitted me for the by-ways of literature like Shakespeare, or the company of the ordinary girls I met, but these I was too shy or too ignorant to compound for, so I read Goethe a few lines at a time with the aid of a translation, or a page from some obscure novel in Spanish, and adored from afar beautiful university girls I should never get to know. Even Turgenev, who became my hero among writers, I read first only because of some novel of his in which there is a description of the Rhineland and German girls passing by in the twilight, murmuring *"Guten Abend."*

This, of course, confined my education mainly to poetry, which has a simpler working vocabulary, based on words like *Herz* and *Schmerz, amour* and *toujours, ardor* and *rumor,* of which I could guess the meaning even when I hadn't a translation. I had taken a checker's discarded notebook from the storage shed, and, having patiently rubbed out all the pencil notes, made a poem book of my own in all the languages I believed I knew. Though my love of poetry sprang from my mother, my taste, I fear, was entirely O'Donovan. Nature would seem to have intended me for an undertaker's assistant, because in any book of verse I read I invariably discovered elegies on dead parents, dead wives, and dead children, and, though my knowledge of poetry expanded, that weakness has persisted, and my favourite poems would be bound to include Bridges' "Perfect Little Body," Landor's "Artemidora, Gods Invisible," De La Mare's mighty poem on the suicide that begins "Steep hung the drowsy street," Hardy's great series on his dead wife, and a mass of Emily Dickinson. And though I was stupid, and went about everything as Father went about putting up a shelf, I did care madly for poetry, good and bad, without understanding why I cared, and coming home at night, still corpse and brass band, I spoke it aloud till people who overheard looked after me in surprise. And this was as it should have been. On the night before his execution at Tyburn Chidiock Tichbourne wrote: "My prime of life is but a frost of cares," and on the night before his in

Kilmainham Patrick Pearse wrote: "The beauty of this world hath made me sad." When life is at its harshest, "when so sad thou can'st not sadder be," poetry comes into its own. Even more than music it is the universal speech, but it is spoken fluently only by those whose existence is already aflame with emotion, for then the beauty and order of language are the only beauty and order possible. Above all, it is the art of the boy and girl overburdened by the troubles of their sex and station, for as Jane Austen so wistfully noted, the difficulty with it is that it can best be appreciated by those who should enjoy it the most sparingly.

It was a strange double life, and small wonder if it comes back to me only as a hallucination. Each morning, as I made my way across the tracks from the passenger station in the early light, I said good-bye to my real self, and at seven that evening when I returned across the dark railway yard and paused in the well-lit passenger station to see the new books and papers in the railway bookstall, he rejoined me, a boy exactly like myself except that no experience had dinged or dented him, and as we went up Mahoney's Avenue in the darkness, we chattered in Irish diversified by quotations in German, French, or Spanish, and talked knowledgeably of Italy and the Rhineland and the beautiful girls one could meet there, and I recited Goethe's poem that in those days was always in my mind—the perfection of the poet's dream of escape:

Kennst du das Land wo die Zitronen blueh'n,
Im dunklem Laub die Goldorangen glueh'n.

I know I often hurt Mother by my moroseness and churlishness when some innocent question of hers brought me tumbling from the heights of language to the English that belonged to the office and the store.

And between Father and myself there was constant friction. Father was a conservative, and he knew the world was full of thieves and murderers. He wouldn't go to bed like a sensible man and let me lock and bolt the doors and quench the lamp. He and Mother might both be burned alive in their beds. But when I went out for an evening walk I hoped frantically to rescue some American heiress whose father would realize the talent that was lost in me, or, failing that, to tag along behind some of the senior members of the Gaelic League and try to talk as grown-up as they seemed, and often and often I wasted my precious couple of hours, walking up and down the Western Road and meeting nobody who would even speak to me. As I came up Summerhill the pleasure of being all of a piece again was overshadowed by the prospect of the morning when once more I should have to part from the half of me that was real, and it was like a blow in the face when I found the door locked, and Mother came scurrying out to open it for me.

"Don't say a word, child!" she would whisper.

"Why?" I would ask defiantly, loud enough to be heard upstairs. "Is he on the war-path again?"

"Ten o'clock that door is locked!" Father would intone from the bedroom.

"Ah, don't answer him! Would you like a cup of tea?"

"Better fed than taught!" Father would add, as he had added any time in the previous ten years.

When my first wretched effort at composition appeared in a children's paper and word of it got round the office, everyone was astonished, but most of all my boss. He was a decent man, and a clever one, and he knew better than anyone that I was definitely not a smart boy. I remember him sitting at his high desk with the paper open before him and a frown on his bulgy forehead as he nervously readjusted his pince-nez.

"Did you write this, Native?"

"Yessir," I said, feeling I had probably done it again. Everything I did only seemed to get me into fresh trouble.

"Nobody help you?"

"No, sir," I replied warily, because it looked as though someone else might get the blame, and I still clung to the code of the boys' weeklies and was always prepared to own up. The frown deepened on his fat face.

"Then for God's sake, stick to writing!" he snapped. "You'll never be any good on the Great Southern and Western Railway."

And that, as we used to say, was one sure five. As usual, looking for models of fine conduct, I had hit on a left-wing time-keeper who knew all the Italian operas by heart and made it a point of honour not to take off his cap before the bosses. Seeing that anyone who knew so much about opera must know the correct thing for other situations, I decided to do the same, with results that may be imagined. Even then, I should probably have been let off with a reprimand, because I had no self-confidence and merely went about blindly imitating anyone and anything, in the hope of blending somehow into the phantasmagoria, but, with my bad sight, I had also fallen over a hand-truck and injured my shin so badly that I couldn't walk for weeks. But on the railway bad sight was more serious than bad manners, because it might result in a claim.

On the Saturday night I was sacked I read my first paper. It was in Irish, and the subject was Goethe. For me, my whole adolescence is summed up in that extraordinary evening—so much that even yet I cannot laugh at it in comfort. I didn't know much about Irish, and I knew practically nothing about Goethe, and that little was wrong. In a truly anthropomorphic spirit I re-created Goethe in my own image and likeness, as a patriotic young man who wished to revive the German language, which I considered to have been gravely threatened by the use of French. I drew an analogy between the French culture that dominated eighteenth-century Germany and the English culture by which we in Ireland were dominated.

While I was speaking, it was suddenly borne in on me that I no longer had a job or a penny in the world, or even a home I could go back to without humiliation, and that the neighbours would say, as they had so often said before, that I was mad and a good-for-nothing. And I knew that they would be right, for here I was committing myself in public to all the vague words and vaguer impressions that with me passed for thought. I could barely control my voice, because the words and impressions no longer meant anything to me. They seemed to come back to me from the rows of polite blank faces as though from the wall of my prison. All that did matter was the act of faith, the hope that somehow, somewhere I would be able to prove that I was neither mad nor a good-for-nothing; because now I realized that whatever it might cost me, there was no turning back. When as kids we came to an orchard wall that seemed too high to climb, we took off our caps and tossed them over the wall, and then we had no choice but to follow them.

I had tossed my cap over the wall of life, and I knew I must follow it, wherever it had fallen.

IV

AFTER AUGHRIM'S GREAT

DISASTER

15

ONCE AGAIN I was without a job. Like the old men whose landladies and daughters-in-law turned them out in the mornings, I made the Public Library my headquarters, and continued to read through the advertisements for a smart boy, though I realized that I was ceasing to be a boy and would probably never be smart. Then I went out and wandered aimlessly about the town in hope of meeting someone who would talk to me, and even maybe give me a cigarette. It was a dreary existence, because Father kept on asking what I was going to do with myself, and I had no notion. It was no use telling him that eventually I hoped to find a job that would suit my peculiar brand of education or meet some rich girl who would recognize my talents and keep me in decent comfort till I established myself. She didn't have to be *very* rich; my needs were simple; only a trousers without a patch on the seat of it, so that I could be seen with her without embarrassment, and an occasional packet of cigarettes. Father, having returned from the War with a disability pension to add to his service pension, was past arguing with—a man who had really set himself up for life!

It was a period of political unrest, and, in a way, this was a relief, because it acted as a safety valve for my own angry emotions. Indeed, it would be truer to say that the Irish nation and myself were both engaged in an elaborate process of improvisation. I was improvising an education I could not afford, and the country was improvising a revolution it could not afford. In 1916 it had risen to a small, real revolution with uniforms and rifles, but the English had brought up artillery that had blown the centre of Dublin flat, and shot down the men in uniform. It was all very like myself and the Christian Brothers. After that, the country had to content itself with a make-believe revolution, and I had to content myself with a make-believe education, and the curious thing is that it was the make-believe that succeeded.

The elected representatives of the Irish people (those who managed to stay out of gaol) elected what they called a government, with a Ministry of Foreign Affairs that tried in vain to get Woodrow Wilson to see it, a Ministry of Finance that exacted five or ten pounds from small shop-keepers who could ill afford it, a Ministry of Defence that tried to buy old-fashioned weapons at outrageous prices from shady characters, and a Ministry of Home Affairs that established courts of justice with part-time Volunteer policemen and no gaols at all.

After Aughrim's Great Disaster

It all began innocently enough. People took to attending Gaelic League concerts at which performers sang "She Is Far from the Land," recited "Let Me Carry Your Cross for Ireland, Lord," or played "The Fox Chase" on the elbow pipes, and armed police broke them up. I remember one that I attended in the town park. When I arrived, the park was already occupied by police, so after a while the crowd began to drift away towards the open country up the river. A mile or so up it re-assembled on the river-bank, but by this time most of the artistes had disappeared. Somebody who knew me asked for a song. At fourteen or fifteen I was delighted by the honour and tried to sing in Irish a seventeenth-century outlaw song about "Sean O'Dwyer of the Valley." I broke down after the first verse—I always did break down whenever I had to make any sort of public appearance because the contrast between what was going on in my head and what was going on in the real world was too much for me—but it didn't matter much. At any moment the police might appear, and this time there could be real bloodshed. It was sheer obstinacy that had driven respectable people to walk miles just to attend a concert they were not very interested in, and they paid their sixpences and went home, rightly feeling that they were the real performers.

It was the same at Mass on Sunday. The bishop, Daniel Coholan—locally known as "Danny Boy"—was a bitter enemy of all this pretence, and every Sunday we had to be ready for a diatribe at Mass. It was as upsetting as discovering that the Invisible Presences still regarded us as traitors, for, though I knew that Ellen Farrell and her husband had defied the Church in Parnell's day, I had had no expectation of ever having to do so. The priest would turn on the altar or ascend the pulpit and start the familiar rigmarole about "defiance of lawful government," and some young man would rise from his seat and move into the nave, genuflect and leave the church. Suddenly every eye would be turned on him, and even the priest would fall silent and wait for the interruption to end. Then there would be a shuffling of feet in one of the aisles, and a girl would rise, genuflect and leave as well. Sometimes this went on for minutes till a considerable group had left. They stood and talked earnestly in the chapel yard, all of them declared rebels, some perhaps marked down for assassination, till the priest finished his harangue and they went back. Naturally, I always joined them, hoping for a nod or a smile from one of them.

It was childish, of course, but so was everything else about the period, like the little grocery shop you saw being re-painted and the name on the fascia board changed from "J. Murphy" to "Sean O'Murchadha." One can still almost date that generation by its Liams, Seans, and Peadars. I suspect that in those few years more books were published in Ireland than in any succeeding twenty years. Not good books, God knows, any more than the little papers that kept on appearing and being suppressed were good papers. But they expressed the mind of the time. One paper I still remember fondly because it proposed that English as a "secondary" language be dropped in favour of French. In those days it struck me as an excellent idea. The impossible, and only the impossible, was law. It was in one way a perfect background for someone like myself who had only the impossible to hope for.

Then the real world began to catch up with the fantasy. The Lord Mayor, Thomas MacCurtain, was murdered by English police in his own home before the eyes of his wife; another Lord Mayor, Terence Mac-

Swiney, was elected in his place and promptly arrested. He went on hunger strike and died in Brixton Gaol. Mother and I were among those who filed past his coffin as he lay in state in the City Hall in his volunteer uniform; the long, dark, masochistic face I had seen only a few months before as he chatted with Corkery by the New Bridge. Years later I talked with a little country shop-keeper from North Cork who had organized a company of Volunteers in his home town, and been so overawed by the tall, dark young man who cycled out from the city to inspect them that he was too shy to ask where MacSwiney was spending the night. Long after, cycling home himself, he saw someone lying in a field by the roadside, and, getting off, found MacSwiney asleep in the wet grass with nothing but an old raincoat round him. That vision of MacSwiney had haunted him through the years of disillusionment.

Curfew was imposed, first at ten, then at five in the afternoon. The bishop excommunicated everyone who supported the use of physical force, but it went on just the same. One night shots were fired on our road and a lorry halted at the top of the square. An English voice kept on screaming hysterically "Oh, my back! my back!" but no one could go out through the wild shooting of panic-stricken men. Soon afterwards the military came in force, and from our back door we saw a red glare mount over the valley of the city. For hours Father, Mother, and I took turns at standing on a chair in the attic, listening to the shooting and watching the whole heart of the city burn. Father was the most upset of us, for he was full of local pride, and ready to take on any misguided foreigner or Dublin jackeen who was not prepared to admit the superiority of Cork over all other cities. Next morning, when I wandered among the ruins, it was not the business district or the municipal buildings that I mourned for, but the handsome red-brick library that had been so much a part of my life from the time when as a small boy I brought back my first Western adventure story over the railway bridges. Later I stood at the corner by Dillon's Cross where the ambush had been and saw a whole block of little houses demolished by a British tank. One had been the home of an old patriot whom my grandparents called "Brienie Dill." A small, silent crowd was held back by soldiers as the tank lumbered across the pavement and thrust at the wall until at last it broke like pie crust and rubble and rafters tumbled. It made a deep impression on me. Always it seemed to be the same thing: the dark, shrunken face of MacSwiney in the candle-light and the wall that burst at the thrust of the tank; "the splendour falls" and "There is no such thing in business as an out-and-out free gift." It was like a symbolic representation of what was always happening to myself, and it seemed as though Ireland did not stand a much better chance. The material world was too strong for both of us.

All the same I could not keep away from Ireland, and I was involved in most of the activities of that imaginative revolution—at a considerable distance, of course, because I was too young, and anyway, I had Father all the time breathing down my neck. In the absence of proper uniform our Army tended to wear riding breeches, gaiters, a trench coat, and a soft hat usually pulled low over one eye, and I managed to scrape up most of the essential equipment, even when I had to beg it, as I begged the pair of broken gaiters from Tom MacKernan. I conducted a complicated deal for the Ministry of Defence and bought a French rifle from a man who lived close to Cork Barrack, though, when I had risked a heavy sentence by bringing it home down

my trouser leg, all the time pretending I had just met
with a serious accident, it turned out that there wasn't
a round of ammunition in Ireland to fit it. When the
British burned and looted Cork and encouraged the
slum-dwellers to join in the looting, I was transferred
to the police and put to searching slums in Blarney
Lane for jewellery and furs. In a back room in Blarney
Lane we located a mink coat which the woman who
lived there said had just been sent her by her sister in
America. Being a polite and unworldly boy of seventeen, I was quite prepared to take her word for it, but
my companion said she hadn't a sister in America, and,
shocked by her untruthfulness, I brought the coat back
to its rightful owners. That she might have needed it
more than they didn't occur to me; I remembered only
that I was now a real policeman, and acted as I felt
a good policeman should act. When Belfast was boy-
cotted during the anti-Catholic pogroms, I was sent
with one or two others to seize a load of Belfast goods
at the station where I had worked a year before. The
Belfast goods mysteriously turned out to be a furniture
van, but you couldn't take me in like that. Belfast busi-
nessmen were very cunning and besides I had my orders. So we made the poor van driver and his horse
trudge all the way to Glanmire, miles down the river,
and only when he opened it up did we realize that it
contained nothing but the furniture of some Catholic family flying from the pogroms.

It was in this atmosphere that I produced my second work, which—as may be understood—was a
translation into Irish of Du Bellay's sonnet, *"Heureux
Qui Comme Ulysse,"* well spoken of in George Wynd-
ham's chatty book on the Pleaide. I was probably deeply
moved by Du Bellay's sentiments, for, being a great
wanderer in my own imagination, I took a deep inter-

est in the feelings of returned travellers. It is probably a recurring fantasy of the provincial, for one friend whom I made later—the most conscientious of officials —never read anything but sea stories, and from Corkery's novel, *The Threshold of Quiet*—itself full of sailors and ships—I can still quote his excellent translation of an inferior French sonnet: "Returned at last from lands we yearn to know."

But this sonnet of mine is another triumph of mind over matter, and, so far as I know, unique in literature, because it is a translation from one language the author didn't know into another that he didn't know— or at best, knew most imperfectly. This was obscured when the poem was published in one of the political weeklies that were always appearing and disappearing as the English caught up with them because *both* languages were even more unknown to editor and printer; and the only thing that could be perceived from the resulting mess was that, whatever the damn thing meant, it must be a sonnet; octet and sestet were unmistakably distinguished. However, a journalist in the *Sunday Independent,* mad with patriotic and linguistic enthusiasm, hailed it as a "perfect translation." It was a period when journalists could improvise a literature as lightly as country clerks improvised government departments. The occasion brought forth the man —a view of history I have always been rather doubtful of.

I haunted the streets for Corkery till I finally trapped him one day by the Scots Church at the foot of Summerhill and casually showed him the cutting from the *Sunday Independent.* He asked if I had the translation with me, and curiously I had that too. He read it carefully with one eye half closed, not commenting too much on the grammar, which was probably invisible through the typographical errors, and said judicially that it *was* a beautiful translation. At any rate, he apparently decided that, since what could not be cured must be endured, he had to admit me to his own little group. After all, I was now a published author.

He lived in a small suburban house on Gardiner's Hill with his mother and sister, surrounded by books and pictures. Over the mantelpiece was a large water colour of his own of a man with a scythe on Fair Hill, overlooking the great panorama of the river valley. Inside the door of the living room was a bust of him by his friend, Joe Higgins, which—if my memory of it is correct—is the only likeness of him that captures all his charm. He presided over his little group from a huge Morris chair with a detachable desk that he had made for himself (he was an excellent craftsman, having been brought up to the trade, and once told me in his oracular way that "nobody had ever met a stupid carpenter," which I later found to be untrue).

He had a good deal of the harshness and puritanism of the provincial intellectual which I share. As those brought up to wealth and rank tend to under-rate them, people accustomed from childhood to an intellectual atmosphere can take classical standards lightly and permit themselves to be entertained by mere facility; not those who have had to buy them dear. Once, when I was working on the railway, and had spent a whole week's pocket money on Wilde's *Intentions,* I met Corkery and he glanced at the book and shook his head. "It'll ruin whatever style you have," he said, and even the suggestion that I might have a style did not make up to me for the realization that once again I had backed the wrong horse.

Most of his friends belonged to a little group that had worked with him when he ran a tiny theatre in

Queen Street. The most faithful visitor was Denis
Breen, a schoolteacher like himself, who had provided
the music and married one of the actresses. He was a
big, emotional man with a fat, sun-coloured face, clear,
childish blue eyes, and a red moustache that he apparently cultivated for the sole purpose of eating it—a
face Franz Hals would have loved. At Gaelic League
meetings he roared down patriotic souls who decried
English music and talked of the greatness of Byrd,
Dowland, and Purcell, whom none of us had ever heard
of. He also professed to be an atheist, which was rather
like proclaiming yourself a Christian in modern China,
and the defensiveness this had induced in him was reflected in everything he did and said. He had a great
contempt for our little colony of German musicians,
whom he spoke of as though they were Catholic priests,
as "bleddy eejits." They, more objectively, spoke of him
as a genius without musical training. It might be fairer
to say that his temperament was too immoderate for
the precise and delicate work of the artist—the very
opposite of Corkery's. The two men were always arguing, Corkery gently and enquiringly, Breen uproariously
and authoritatively, something like this. "Well, on the
other hand, would it not be possible to say . . . ?" "Me
dear man, it's possible to say anything, if you're fool
enough." I listened in shame for the whole human race
to think that anyone could be so presumptuous as to
disagree with Corkery.

I did not like Breen. I was connected with him
through two coincidences: one that he had taught me
for a couple of days before I left Blarney Lane for good,
and even in that short time he had beaten me (Irish
teachers, like American policemen, never having
learned that to go about armed is not the best way of
securing obedience and respect); the other was that

my mother and his mother, who kept a little sweet shop at the gate of the University, had been friends. *His* mother had told *my* mother that even when he was a small boy no one could control him. He would get hungry at night, go down to the shop for biscuits, sample every tin and leave them all open, so that by morning her stock was ruined. Even when I knew him he would begin his tea by eating all the sweet cakes in case anyone else took a fancy to them. He was greedy with a child's greed, shouted everyone down with what he thought "funny" stories or denunciations of the "bleddy eejits" who ran the country or its music, and battered a Beethoven sonata to death with his red eyebrows reverently raised, believing himself to be a man of perfect manners, liberal ideas, and perfect taste. All of which, of course, he was, as I learned later when we became friends, for though his wife and my mother would look blank while he ate all the confectionery and then shouted for more; and though afterwards he hammered Wolf's *An Die Geliebte* unconscious; he struck out the last chords as only a man who loved music could do it, scowling and muttering: "Now listen to the bloody stars!" He quarreled bitterly with me after the first performance of a play called *The Invincibles* because he had convinced himself that I had caricatured him in the part of Joe Brady, the leader of the assassins—a brave and simple man driven mad by injustice—and though at the time I was disturbed because such an idea had never occurred to me, it seems to me now that the characters in whom we think we recognize ourselves are infinitely more revealing of our real personalities than those in which someone actually attempts to portray us.

But Corkery's greatest friend was Sean O'Faolain, who was three years older than I and all the things I should have wished to be—handsome, brilliant, and, above all, industrious. For Corkery, who loved application, kept on rubbing it in that I didn't work as O'Faolain did. Once the three of us met on Patrick's Bridge after Corkery and O'Faolain had attended a service at the cathedral, and when O'Faolain went off in his home-spun suit, swinging his ash-plant, Corkery looked after him as I had once seen him look after Terence MacSwiney and said: "There goes a born literary man!" For months I was mad with jealousy.

The first book I took from Corkery's bookcase was a Browning. It was characteristic of my topsy-turvy self-education that I knew by heart thousands of lines in German and Irish, without really knowing either language, but had never heard of Browning, or indeed of any other English poet but Shakespeare, whom I didn't think much of. But my trouble with poetry was that of most auto-didacts. I could not afford books, so I copied and memorized like mad. It is a theory among scholars that all great periods of manuscript activity coincide with some impending social disaster and that scribes are like poor Jews in the midst of a hostile community, gathering up their few little treasures in the most portable form before the next pogrom. Obviously I anticipated the disaster of the Irish Civil War, because I never seemed to possess anything unless I had written it down and learned it by heart, and though I scorned what I thought mediocre verse, and never bothered to acquire anything that had not been approved by the best authorities, the authorities themselves proved most unreliable, and for every good poem I learned, I learned six bad ones. Unlike the poor Jew, I could not throw away the imitation pearls, so, though my taste in poetry improved, my memory refused to adapt itself, and when it should have been producing masterpieces, it would suddenly take things into its own hands and produce something frightful by some minor Georgian poet like Drinkwater. Describing the death of a neighbour, a small boy in our locality drew his hand across his throat and said darkly: "De woman went before her God full up to *dat* of whisky." I shall go before mine full up to *that* of bad poetry.

Music was different and much more difficult because I had no standards at all. When people played or sang music-hall songs I behaved as I did when they told dirty stories and either left the room or read a book, but I could not go out in the evening without passing a neighbour's house where an old-fashioned horn-gramophone bellowed songs from *The Arcadians* and, in spite of the fact that the Christian Brothers thought I had a defective ear, I picked them up and—like the bad poetry—I have them still. When I became friends with a young fellow called Tom MacKernan, who drilled beside me in the Volunteers and played the fiddle, I got him to play me certified classical tunes from his violin book. I even got him to lend me an old fiddle and a tutor, but I could not make head or tail of staff notation. When I met Jack Hendrick, whose brother was a singer, I got him to teach me the songs his brother sang at musical competitions like "Where'er You Walk" and *"Am Stillen Herd,"* though I still could not understand key changes and thought he was probably singing out of tune. Corkery took me a couple of times to real piano recitals by Tilly Fleischmann and Geraldine Sullivan, but, though I read the programme notes like mad—they were usually by Corkery's friend, Father Pat MacSwiney—and pretended to myself that I could recognize the moment when "the dawn wind wakes the sleeping leaves, and these, tapping at the window pane, rouse the joyous maiden who has been dreaming of her secret lover," it always turned out that I had just been listening to the climax in which "Smiling, she leans through the window and plucks a rose for her hair." It mortified me to see all those educated people who had no difficulty in distinguishing the dawn wind rising from a girl plucking a rose for her hair and made me feel that life was really unfair.

I had no luck with music till Corkery bought a gramophone from Germany immediately after the 1914–1918 War, when the rate of exchange was favourable, and with it a selection of records that included Bach's Sixth Cello Sonata, a couple of Beethoven symphonies, Mozart's Violin Concerto in A, Schubert's "Unfinished" and Strauss's *Till Eulenspiegel.* I gave Strauss up as a bad job because it would clearly not be portable in any future pogrom, but I practically learned the Seventh Symphony and the Mozart Concerto by heart, and for years judged everything by them. I can now read second-rate books without getting sick, but I still cannot listen to mediocre music. I had too much trouble escaping from it.

Corkery took me sketching with him as well, but I was never much good at that; "it's like me with my game leg entering for the hundred yards," he said kindly, blaming it on my sight, but it wasn't my sight. It was my undeveloped visual sense. The imagination, because it is by its nature subjective, pitches first on the area of the intimate arts—poetry and music. Painting, which is more objective and critical, comes later. Still, that did not keep him from getting me into the School of Art, where I spent my time copying casts, drawing from the male model, and arguing like mad with my teacher, who said that Michelangelo was "very coarse." Apparently, Corkery's idea was that since I could never get into a university, I should become an art teacher, and he even arranged a scholarship in London for me. But I was in a frenzy to earn a little money, and, instead, like a fool, I applied for a scholarship to a Gaelic League Summer School in Dublin that had been formed to train teachers of Irish, who would later cycle about the country from village to village, teaching in schools and parish halls. It sounded exactly the sort of life for an aspiring young writer who wanted to know Ireland as Gorky had known Russia.

The Summer School was held in the Gaelic League headquarters in Parnell Square, and the head of it was a sly, fat rogue of a West Cork man called Hurley, who was later Quarter-Master General of the Free State Army. I did not like Dublin, probably because most of the time I was light-headed with hunger. I lodged in a Georgian house on the Pembroke Road, and, having rarely eaten in any house other than my own, I contented myself with a cup of tea and a slice of bread for breakfast. I decided that the chamber pot in my bedroom was for ornament rather than use. I was even more scared of restaurants than of strange houses. I had never eaten in one except when Mother took me to Thompson's café in Patrick Street for a cup of coffee —her notion of high life—so I lived entirely on coffee and buns in Bewley's. It was to be years before I worked up the courage to go into a real restaurant. Besides, the scholarship did not amount to more than the price of modest lodgings, and I needed every penny I could spare for the books I could pick up cheap at the stalls on the quays. I could not keep away from them. There were books there the like of which one never saw in a Cork bookstore. It was there that I picked up for a few pence the little *Selected Poems of Browning* published by Smith, Elder, which for me has always been one of the great books of the world, and when the hunger got too much for me I would recite to myself: "Heap cassia, sandal-buds and stripes of labdanum and aloeballs" as though it were a spell.

Far from being recognized as a genius at the school, I was obviously regarded as a complete dud. The reason for this did not dawn on me till years had gone by. All the other students had had a good general education, some a university education. I talked Irish copiously, but nobody had explained to me the difference between a masculine and feminine noun, or a nominative and dative case. Nobody explained to me then either, probably because the problem of a completely uneducated boy masquerading as a well-educated one was outside everyone's experience.

And yet, the whole country was doing the same, and Hurley, who gave the impression of having served his time in a West Cork drapery store, was on his way to one of the highest ranks in the army. My friends in the school were a Dubliner called Byrne and a Kerryman called Kavanagh. Byrne was doubly endeared to me because, though only a boy scout, he had already been involved in a pistol fight with a police patrol. Some hunger striker had died in prison and was being given a public funeral, so the three of us demanded the afternoon off to attend it, and fell foul of Hurley, who objected to what he called "politics" in the school. When the time for the funeral came the three of us got up to leave the class, and Hurley, in a rage, dismissed it. We were expecting trouble, and Byrne had a revolver. The imaginary revolution was taking shape as well.

I was lucky to return to Cork with a certificate that made me a qualified teacher of Irish—which I was not —and for a few weeks I cycled eight or ten miles out of the city in the evenings to teach in country schools by lamp-light. But already even this was becoming dangerous, and soon curfew put an end to my new career as well. I seemed to be very unlucky with my jobs.

At the same time I was making friends of a different type. One evening a pale, thin-lipped young clerk in an insurance office called Jack Hendrick came to see me with an introduction from Corkery and proposed that the two of us should start a literary and debating society. Our conversation was rather at cross-purposes, for he did not seem to have read anything but D'Israeli's *Curiosities of Literature* and he continued to quote this to me as I quoted Turgenev and Dostoevsky to him. He didn't seem to know about them, and I had never heard of D'Israeli, so I agreed to borrow it from him and meanwhile lent him Turgenev's *Virgin Soil* and Gogol's *Taras Bulba*. When we met again I admitted that I was bored with D'Israeli, and he said he thought Turgenev was "cold." We didn't seem to be getting anywhere, but I needed a friend too badly to reject one merely because he said outrageous things about Turgenev, and Hendrick was exactly the sort of friend I needed because he had every virtue that I lacked and was well-mannered, methodical, cool, and thoughtful. He had a neat, square, erect handwriting that I greatly admired for its legibility, and I set out to imitate it as I had imitated Corkery's monosyllabic articulation, but I was too restive to do anything that required exacting labour, and Hendrick's handwriting was a career in itself.

I explained to him that I now had a chance of a teaching job, but it meant I would have to ride a bicycle, and I had been assured by the man who had tried to teach me that I had no sense of balance and would never be able to ride. I had accepted this without question because it was only one of the dozen things I had been told I couldn't do. I couldn't sing; I couldn't pass an examination; I couldn't persevere at a task—naturally I couldn't ride a bicycle. That evening Hendrick brought his sister's bicycle out the Ballyvolane Road, put me up on it, unclenched my fists on the handle-bars, and when we came to the first long hill, gave me a push that sent me flying. I was a mass of bruises when I picked myself up at the foot of the hill, but when I had wheeled back the bicycle, Hendrick, who by this time was sitting on the grass by the roadside, smoking, took out his cigarettes and said with a pale smile: "Now you know how to ride a bicycle."

But even this was of less importance to me than the fact that I was beginning to make friends away from my own gas-lamp. It was probably this that Blake had in mind when he said that if only a fool would persevere in his folly he would become a wise man, because sooner or later the imaginative improvisation imposes itself on reality. But it is only then that its real troubles begin, when it must learn to restrain itself from imposing too far, and acquire a smattering of the practical sense it has rejected. That, I think, is where the Irish Revolution broke down. The imagination is a refrigerator, not an incubator; it preserves the personality intact through disaster after disaster, but even when it has changed the whole world it has still changed nothing in itself and emerges as a sort of Rip Van Winkle, older in years but not in experience. This sets up a time lag that can never be really overcome.

Friendship did not make me wiser or happier, for years of lonely day-dreaming had left me emotionally at the age of ten. I was ashamed to admit that there was anything I didn't know, and one evening when Corkery talked to me about a story of Gorky's in which there was a eunuch, I was too mortified to admit that I didn't know what a eunuch was. I was morbidly sensitive, jealous, exacting, and terrified of strangers. I did not merely make friends; I fell in love, and even the suspicion of a slight left me as frantic as a neurotic schoolgirl. The attitudes of the ghetto survive emancipation, and I had only to enter a strange house or talk to a stranger to make a complete fool of myself. From excessive shyness I always talked too much, usually lost control of myself, and heard myself say things that were ridiculous, false, or base, and afterwards remained awake, raging and sobbing by turns as I remembered every detail of my own awkwardness, lying, and treachery. Years later, when I was earning money, I never went to a strange house without first taking a drink or two to brace me for the ordeal. Whether that was much help or not I do not know. It is enough that the things I said when I was slightly intoxicated were never quite as bad as the things I said when I wasn't.

As if this weren't enough, I was also going through the usual adolescent phase of snobbery and was ashamed of my parents, ashamed of the little house where we lived, and when people called for me, I grabbed my cap and dragged them out anywhere, for fear Father should start telling funny stories about his army days or Mother reveal that she was only a charwoman. With me, of course, this was also complicated by the number of things that really humiliated me, like my clothes, which were decent but patched, and the fact that I could never get on a tram without first scanning the passengers to make sure there was no girl aboard whose fare I should not be able to pay. As a result I never got on a tram at all until the moment it started to move, and tried to find a seat where no one could come and sit beside me. Then if I continued to look out at the street till the conductor had gone by, I was safe.

My fight for Irish freedom was of the same order

as my fight for other sorts of freedom. Still like Dolan's ass, I went a bit of the way with everybody, and in those days everybody was moving in the same direction. Hendrick did not get me to join a debating society, but I got him to join the Volunteers. If it was nothing else, it was a brief escape from tedium and frustration to go out the country roads on summer evenings, slouching along in knee breeches and gaiters, hands in the pockets of one's trench-coat and hat pulled over one's right eye. Usually it was only to a parade in some field with high fences off the Rathcooney Road, but sometimes it was a barrack that was being attacked, and we trenched roads and felled trees, and then went home through the wet fields over the hills, listening for distant explosions and scanning the horizon for fires. It was all too much for poor Father, who had already seen me waste my time making toy theatres when I should have been playing football, and drawing naked men when I should have been earning my living. And this time he did at least know what he was talking about. For all he knew I might have the makings of a painter or writer in me, but, as an old soldier himself, he knew that I would never draw even a disability pension. No good could come of such foolishness, and it would only be the mercy of God if the police at St. Luke's didn't blame him for my conduct and write to the War Office to get his pensions stopped. The old trouble about locking the door at night became acute. Ten o'clock was when he went to bed—earlier when curfew was on— and the door had to be fastened for the night: the latch, the lock, the big bolt, and the little bolt. When I knocked, Mother got out of bed to open it, Father shouted at her, and she called back indignantly to him not to wake the neighbours, and whispered in anguish to me: "Don't answer him whatever he says!" But stung in my pride as a soldier of Ireland, I often did answer back, and then he roared louder than ever that I was "better fed than taught." Mother's sympathies were entirely with the revolution, and he would have been more furious still if he had known that not long after she was doing odd errands herself, carrying revolvers and despatches. Or maybe he did know, and, like many another husband, decided to ignore her minor infidelities.

I was changing, but though I did not realize it till much later, Corkery was changing too, in an infinitely subtler and more significant way, and the man I loved was turning into someone I should not even be able to understand. I was merely puzzled and hurt when one night he said: "You must remember there are more important things in life than literature." I knew there weren't, because if there were I should be doing them. That change goes farther back than the period I am writing of, and was not perceptible until years later. It is not in his novel, *The Threshold of Quiet,* but it is already adumbrated in the first story of *A Munster Twilight*. In this a worldly farmer wishes to plough the Ridge of the Saints—sanctified ground—but his old farmhand, steeped in traditional pieties, refuses to do it. He taunts his employer by offering to plough the Ridge if the farmer will put his great sire-horse, Ember, to the plough. At the end of the story the old farmhand yokes the sire-horse and the mare, whose name is Beauty, and goes out at nightfall to plough the Ridge, the horses quarrel and horses and man are hurled together over the cliff.

This is a typical bit of symbolism that seems to sum up a deep personal conflict. It describes the suicidal destruction of the creative faculty as an act of revolt against the worldliness of everyday life. "There are more important things in life than literature." Scores of other modern writers like Ibsen and James have used such symbolic equations as a way of trying out their personal problems, but this one seems to me to describe what really happened. It is as though the imaginative improvisation of the community had begun to dominate the imaginative improvisation of the artist and make its fires seem dim by comparison. Of course there must have been some more immediate cause, and I sometimes wonder whether it was not Corkery's friendship with Thomas MacCurtain and Terence MacSwiney. MacCurtain's murder aroused the country and MacSwiney's death on hunger-strike was watched by the whole world and cost the British Government more than a major military defeat. It seems to me now that Corkery's admiration for the two men may have made him feel that men of action had more to give than the mere artist like himself. His admiration for the men of action is in *The Hounds of Banba*, the book of stories he was writing at the time, and there are stories in this that repeat the symbolic equation of the horses. One, for instance, describes how a jockey, who is also a traditionalist, takes up a bet made by his half-witted employer, rides a famous horse along the cliffs, and then wrestles with the horse and throws him bodily over the edge into the sea. Even in the stories where there is no symbolism there is a celebration of imaginary heroes and an attack on imaginary enemies who are not far removed from windmills. And Corkery knew his windmill-fighters, for once when we were looking at a picture called *Don Quixote* he said sharply: "Those eyes are wrong. They're looking out. Quixote's eyes looked inward."

I do not blame myself for not understanding and sympathizing with what was happening to him, because it was precisely the opposite of what was happening to me. He was a man who, by force of character, had dominated physical difficulties, family circumstances, and a provincial environment that would have broken down anyone but a great man. Breen, who gave the impression of being opposed to him, cursed and raged whenever he described Corkery's suffering in the teachers' training college they had attended together, and I am certain that this sprang from Breen's own clear eye and passionate heart rather than from any self-pity on Corkery's part. Nowadays I remember how his mind seemed always to brood on self-control, as when he described how he had written his novel, getting up each morning at six, or wrote to me when I was in prison, quoting Keats on the beneficial effect of a shave and wash-up when one's spirits were low, or praised Michael Collins, who had made himself leader of the whole revolutionary movement because he was up answering letters when everyone else was in bed. He was as shy and reserved as Chekhov and never asked for sympathy, but behind words like these one could detect a whole lifetime of self-control. Yet he did not, as a lesser man might have done, lose generosity in speaking of an enemy or gentleness in rebuking a friend. He would gaze at me gloomily, and predict in his harsh, unmodulated voice that I would go through life without ever finishing anything, and then add "like Coleridge," awarding me a valuable second prize. I have described how he ticked me off for reading Wilde, because it would injure whatever style I had. Yeats had exactly the same trick. When he was forming his Academy, even before I had published a book, he and I quarrelled about the constitution of the Academy and he muttered: "Why worry about literary eminence? You and I will provide that." Of course it was guileful, and in a lesser man it might have been the basest flattery, but I understood it in him as in Corkery as the desperate attempt of the elderly and eminent man to break down the barriers that separated him from youth and awkwardness. Because of that Corkery developed an authority that was like Yeats's. If, as I now fancy, he was impressed by MacSwiney's sacrifice, it was probably because MacSwiney's remarkable self-control and self-denial had given him an authority beyond his intellect and gifts, but Corkery's self-control was of a rarer kind. However little he said, and however insipid what he said might seem, it was on his judgement that we all relied, and I think that in the way of those who combine self-control and humanity, austerity and sweetness, he was full of a consciousness of his own power he would have been much too shy to reveal. Only once did he let anything drop that suggested it, and that was one evening when I suggested that great writers might be more careful of what they did and said if only they remembered the sort of people who would write their lives, and he shrugged and replied: "Well, I know people will write my life. . . ."

That is the period when I best like to remember him. After a cruel day's teaching he would take his paints and sketch-book and trudge miles into the country with me at his heels. I would quote a line or two of Omar Khayyám, and at once he would take alarm lest any fledgeling of his should be taken in by something less than a masterpiece. "What *is* it about Fitzgerald that's not quite right?" he would ask, and I, as well-skilled in the responses as any acolyte, would reply: "Well, it is a bit sugary, isn't it?" "It is on the sweet side," he would say thoughtfully, as though the idea had only just occurred to him, and then, seeing the gable of a cottage in the evening light, he would climb laboriously over a stone wall and search for a dry stone to sit on, cracking jokes about his own softness. "Turner, of course, sat in a wet ditch to paint." Then, in the late evening he stood at the door of his little house, leaning against the jamb to take the weight from off his bad foot, his hands in his trousers pockets and his small, dark, handsome head thrown lazily back as he talked endlessly about writers and writing, lost to everything else, a man mad on literature. And remembering him like this I find myself humming the song I made Hendrick teach me: *Herr Walther von der Vogelweid, der ist mein Meister gewesen.*

But self-control like his exacts a terrible price from the artist, and already, like the king in his own play, weary of struggle with the world, he must have been brooding on abdication before those who seemed to exercise real authority, even though it could never be more than a shadow of his own.

16

THEN CAME the Truce. It was an extraordinary event that deserves a whole book to itself, though, so far as I know, no one has even tried to describe it. It had all been announced and prepared for, but it was quite impossible to believe it would really happen. Then, a little before noon on Monday, July 11, 1921, when I was still a few months short of eighteen, a slow procession of armoured cars, tanks, and patrols began to move back on Cork Barracks, and I walked along beside it. There were little crowds in every street, all watchful and silent, since everyone realized that anything might yet happen. Then, as the Angelus rang out from the city churches, the barrack gates were thrown open and tanks, armoured cars, officers, and men filed in. Here and there a man would turn and give a derisive hoot at the silent crowd. Then the barrack gates closed, and the crowd began to move away quietly with bewildered looks. Did it really mean that it was all over? That there would be no more five o'clock curfew and that one could walk that night as late as one pleased without being shot? That one could sleep in one's own bed? That it really represented the end of seven hundred years of military occupation, the triumph of the imagination over material power, the impossible become law?

All that perfect summer young men who had been for years in hiding drove about the country in commandeered cars, drinking, dancing, brandishing their guns. In the evenings the local Volunteers, their numbers vastly increased by careful young men who were now beginning to think that after all there might be something in this for them, drilled openly and learned how to use rifles and machine guns.

And then, in the depth of winter, came the Treaty with England, which granted us everything we had ever sought except an independent republican government and control of the loyalist province of Ulster. The withholding of these precipitated a Civil War, which, in the light of what we know now, might have been anticipated by anyone with sense, for it was merely an extension into the fourth dimension of the improvisation that had begun after the crushing of the insurrection in 1916. The Nationalist movement had split up into the Free State Party, who accepted the treaty with England and the Republicans who opposed it by force of arms, as the Irgun was to do much later in Israel. Ireland had improvised a government, and clearly no government that claimed even a fraction less than the imaginary government had claimed could attract the loyalty of young men and women with imagination.

They were like a theatre audience that, having learned to dispense with fortuitous properties, lighting, and scenery and begun to appreciate theatre in the raw, were being asked to content themselves with cardboard and canvas. Where there is nothing, there is reality.

But meanwhile the improvisation had cracked: the English could have cracked it much sooner merely by yielding a little to it. When, after election results had shown that a majority of the people wanted the compromise—and when would *they* not have accepted a compromise?—our side continued to maintain that the only real government was the imaginary one, or the few shadowy figures that remained of it, we were acting on the unimpeachable logic of the imagination, that only what exists in the mind is real. What we ignored was that a whole section of the improvisation had cut itself adrift and become a new and more menacing reality. The explosion of the dialectic, the sudden violent emergence of thesis and antithesis from the old synthesis, had occurred under our very noses and we could not see it or control it. Rory O'Connor and Mellowes in seizing the Four Courts were merely echoing Patrick Pearse and the seizure of the Post Office, and Michael Collins, who could so easily have starved them out with a few pickets, imitated the English pattern by blasting the Four Courts with borrowed artillery. And what neither group saw was that every word we said, every act we committed, was a destruction of the improvisation and what we were bringing about was a new Establishment of Church and State in which imagination would play no part, and young men and women would emigrate to the ends of the earth, not because the country was poor, but because it was mediocre.

To say that I took the wrong side would promote

me to a degree of intelligence I had not reached. I took
the Republican side because it was Corkery's. Breen
was going round in a fury, saying we were all "bleddy
eejits," as though we were no better than Catholic
priests or German musicians, and O'Faolain shared his
views. I still saw life through a veil of literature—the
only sort of detachment available to me—though the
passion for poetry was merging into a passion for
the nineteenth-century novel, and I was tending to
see the Bad Girl of the neighbourhood not as "one more
unfortunate" but as Madame Bovary or Nastasya
Filipovna, and the Western Road—the evening prom-
enade of clerks and shop-girls—as the Nevsky Prospekt.

In such a set-up it was only natural that Hendrick
and I should be installed as censors of the local newspaper, and, as we had no real news, compelled to fill it
with bad patriotic verse by our superiors, who had a
passion for writing about the woes of dear old Ireland.
It was a great triumph when O'Faolain walked in one
night and gave us a good poem, for it seemed as if the
right people were coming round. It was also only natural that I, on the basis of an intimate acquaintance
with Tolstoy's *Sebastopol*, should be cast for the part of
war correspondent. It was a shock for us both when
one day one of the Dublin publicity people walked into
the office and took an agency message we were printing, describing a raid on the house of Mrs. Pearse, and
re-wrote it under our eyes as: "Great indignation has
been expressed in Dublin at the raiding of the house of
Mrs. Pearse, the widowed mother of the martyred Irish
leader, P. H. Pearse." It was clear to us that in some
ways the Dublin group were much cleverer than we.

This was how we came to meet Erskine Childers,
one of the great romantic figures of the period—a distinguished British officer with Irish family connections

who had written a remarkably prophetic thriller that anticipated the First World War and, after it ended, returned to Ireland to serve the Irish cause. Our first glimpse of him was disappointing. He came down the stairs of the Victoria Hotel, limping and frowning; a small, slight, grey-haired man in tweeds with a tweed cap pulled over his eyes, wearing a light mackintosh stuffed with papers and carrying another coat over his arm. Apart from his accent, which would have identified him anywhere, there was something peculiarly English about him; something that nowadays reminds me of some old parson or public-school teacher I have known, conscientious to a fault and overburdened with minor cares. His thin, grey face, shrunk almost to its mould of bone, had a coldness as though life had contracted behind it to its narrowest span; the brows were puckered in a triangle of obsessive thought like pain, and the eyes were clear, pale, and tragic. "All sicklied o'er with the pale cast of thought," Corkery quoted after he met him. Later, Childers's friend, George Russell, asked me if I thought he was taking drugs. I was certain he wasn't, but I knew what Russell meant, for I have seen a look exactly like that on the faces of drug addicts.

We went down Patrick Street towards our headquarters on the Grand Parade, and half-way there Childers paused and frowned. He had been instructed to register under a false name at the hotel, but had he remembered to do so or given his own name by mistake? I returned to the hotel to check, and, sure enough, he had registered as Mr. Smith—Mr. John Smith, I feel sure. Later, in our headquarters, we showed him the local political paper that O'Faolain was producing at his own expense, and he passed indifferently over my poem and Hendrick's sketch, and lit with what seemed an inspired lack of taste on O'Faolain's article, "Khaki or Green?" which, for him, put the whole political situation into a slogan. It was a trick I was to notice in him again and again, and it left me disillusioned. This was a sort of mind I had never met before.

A day or two later Hendrick and I, coming back to work, noticed him drifting aimlessly along King Street, his hands deep in the pockets of his mackintosh. It amused us to watch the way he stopped and started again. Once he stopped to stare in a shop-window that, when we reached it, turned out to be full of women's underclothes. He had a sort of doddering, drooping absent-mindedness that at times resembled that of a parson in a comedy. We had been following him for a few minutes when we noticed that someone else was doing the same. This was a shabbily dressed man who seemed to have little experience of following anybody. When Childers stopped and looked in a shop-window he did so too. When Childers went on he went on, following step by step.

Knowing Cork as we did, we had no difficulty in getting ahead of them both, and as Childers passed the laneway into the English Market, we pulled him in, told him what was happening, and asked for his gun. He was very alarmed at our manner, but with old-fashioned politeness he turned aside, unbuttoned one mackintosh, then another, then a jacket, and finally a vest. Just over his heart and fixed to his braces by a safety pin was a tiny delicately made gun such as a middle-aged lady of timid disposition might carry in her handbag.

We waited to let the shadow pick him up again, and then we picked up the shadow and took him up another lane off the South Mall. As a spy he was not much good, but as interrogators we were worse, and we let him go when we had taken his name and address and given him a talking-to. Besides, we didn't take it seriously. It wasn't until weeks later that we found out that Childers—"the damned Englishman," as Griffith had called him—was the one man the Provisional Government was bent on killing.

When we returned the toy gun to Childers he looked happy for the first time since we had met him. He had not worried himself about being shadowed but was concerned for the loss of his gun and drove the other people in the office distracted enquiring whether Hendrick and I were responsible enough to be entrusted with it. He pinned it back on his braces as if it was a flower he was pinning to his buttonhole and told us in the dry tone that Englishmen reserve for intimate revelations that it was a present from a friend. Someone told me later that the friend was Michael Collins, the enemy Commander-in-Chief. True or not, that was certainly in character.

I accompanied him soon after to General Headquarters in Fermoy. It was a bright summer morning, and I still remember how I first saw the mountains over Mitchelstown in a frame of wayside trees and felt that at last I was going to see something of Ireland. We stood in the barrack square at Fermoy and saw the generals emerge from a staff meeting, some in uniform, others in civilian clothes with bandoleers and belts. One carried a Lewis gun over his shoulder—a general cannot be too careful. Afterwards we had lunch in the Officers' Mess. Liam Lynch presided in uniform, looking like the superior of an enclosed order in disguise. The meal was a strange mixture of awkwardness and heartiness such as went on in officers' messes on the enemy side when local tradesmen and clerks sat down to dinner in quarters they had once approached by the serv-

ants' entrance. That night Childers fixed a bedside
lamp for himself so that it would not interfere with
the pair of us who shared his room, and when I woke
during the night he was still reading and trying to
smother a persistent cough so as not to wake us. He was
reading *Twenty Years After*. I was reading *The Idiot*
and felt sorry that he did not read more improving
books. Though I had cast myself for the part of Tolstoy
at Sebastopol, I was going through a phase that favoured Dostoevsky and Whitman.

Next night I found myself in Ashill Towers near
Kilmallock, a pseudo-Gothic castle that we had taken
over as headquarters for our front line. If only I had
realized it, it was here that the genius of improvisation
had taken complete charge. In Buttevant and Fermoy
we had real military barracks, complete with officers'
messes; we had an armoured car—a most improbable-
looking vehicle, like the plywood tank that captured a
Chinese town where a friend was living, flying a large
streamer that read "Particularly Fierce Tank." We
even had a Big Gun that had been made by a Dubliner
who had brought it with him to Buttevant along with
the nine shells he had made for it and the tenth that
was still in process of construction. But the front line
was our pride and joy. We had improvised almost
everything else but never a front line. The enemy were
reported to be on the point of attacking it, and in the
library the local officers were hard at work over their
maps deciding which bridges to blow up in the track of
their advance.

In the long Gothic hall there were fifty or sixty
men at either side of the long trestle tables in the candle-light, their rifles slung over their shoulders. The
hall seemed to tremble with the flickering of the candles, and tusked and antlered heads peered down from

the half-darkness as though even they couldn't believe what they were seeing. Suddenly a young man sprang on a table with a rifle in his hand and sang Canon Sheehan's romantic version of the old outlaw song of Sean O'Dwyer of the Valley. He had a fine untrained Irish tenor, with the vibrant, almost exasperating emotional quality of the pure head voice.

> *After Aughrim's great disaster,*
> *When the foe in sooth was master,*
> *It was you who first plunged in and swam*
> *The Shannon's boiling flood. . . .*

In the early morning, with the news of enemy movements all along the front, I was sent with a char-a-banc to bring reinforcements from Croom. That, too, thrilled me, because I knew that Croom was an old fortress of the O'Donovans from which we had been expelled in the twelfth century by Donal O'Brien. There was a red glow in the sky as I went from house to house in the little town, hammering on the doors with the butt of a carbine which somebody had given me to keep me happy. When I had brought back the reinforcements I was sent to Divisional Headquarters in Buttevant with despatches for the Divisional Commander, Liam Deasy, but he disappointed all my expectations by ignoring the despatches, telling me I looked very tired, and putting me to bed in his own room. He was the kindest man I'd met in my short military experience, and to be put to bed by the General was as much as any young Cherubino could ask, but I wasn't satisfied. It struck me that the General wasn't taking the despatches seriously enough, and after a couple of sleepless hours I went out into the barrack square to look for him. I wasn't the only one who was doing it. There was a column of men lined up there—the angriest-looking men I'd ever seen—and their officer asked me where General Deasy was. I didn't know, I said; I was just looking for him myself. "Well, when you find him, tell him we're the Limerick column," the officer said. "We're after fighting our way down from Patrickswell, and when we got here the Corkmen had meat for their breakfast and we had none. Tell him if the Limerick men don't get meat there'll be mutiny."

I found Deasy on his way from Mass and he took the news of the possible mutiny as calmly as he'd taken the news of the expected assault on the front line. He gave me despatches for Kilmallock, and warned me urgently to check with the officer in charge at Charleville to make sure there were no enemy troops between me and the front. I took this as a rather fussy precaution dictated by the importance of the despatches, but afterwards I wondered if the General had quite as much faith in our front line as everyone else seemed to have.

It was a sunny summer morning, and on my way I picked up a little hunchback wearing a Red Cross armlet who was making his way to the front on foot, apparently on the off-chance that there might be scope there for an enterprising one-man medical service. At the time that struck me as the most natural thing in the world, whereas nowadays I merely wonder what revelation had been given that little hunchback in whatever back lane he came from to send him trudging off by himself on the roads of Ireland, looking for a battlefield where he might come in useful.

At Charleville I checked with the local commandant. He was still in bed but he assured me that there wasn't an enemy soldier within miles. What he failed to remember was that it was Sunday, and on Sunday the whole Irish race is unanimously moved to go to Mass, so that at that very moment our whole nine-mile front, pickets, machine-gun posts, fortresses and all, had simply melted away, and there wasn't as much as a fallen tree between me and the enemy. In itself that mightn't have been too bad because it might also be assumed that there wouldn't be any enemy pickets either; but a considerable number of the enemy facing us were from the neighbourhood of Charleville, and after his longing for Mass, an Irishman's strongest characteristic is his longing for home and Mother, and anyone who knew his Ireland would have guessed that on that fine summer morning our whole front was being pierced in a dozen places by nostalgic enemy soldiers, alone or in force, all pining to embrace their mothers and discover if the cow had calved.

Just before the real trouble began I saw the people coming from Mass in a small wayside church. They looked curiously at the car, and I thought how peaceful it all was, the flat, green country and the tall sunshot hedges and the people coming from Mass in their Sunday clothes. And then men in half-uniform emerged from the hedges, levelling their rifles at us and signalling us on. I wasn't worried; I knew they must be our own men, but my driver hissed "Eat them!" obviously referring to the despatches, and I guessed I must be wrong. He had probably seen despatches eaten in the movies, because even a horse couldn't have got down Deasy's despatches in the minute or two that remained to me, so I tore them up and scattered them. In the high wind they blew across the fields beyond retrieving. Then we reached a road block manned by an officer and half a dozen men and were stopped. I had left my carbine in Ashill Towers and had nothing but my camera and *The Idiot*. The camera was taken though the book was returned. The officer was stupid, truculent, and

argumentative, and my temper was in a shocking state.
It had just dawned on me that on my first day in action
I had allowed myself to be made prisoner, that a brilliant career as war correspondent had been closed to
me, and that the front line might sway to and fro for
years in great battles like those of the First World War
but that someone else would be its Tolstoy. When he
said something nasty I called him and his men a gang
of traitors. It was typical of things at the time that I
could say it and get away with it. Six months later, it
would have been very different. Just then everyone
had a slightly bewildered air as though he were wondering how on earth such things could happen to *him*.
After all, it is not every day that the dialectic blows up
in your face and you, who have always regarded yourself as the victim, wake up to find yourself the tyrant.

The enemy headquarters was in a farmhouse a
few hundred yards down a by-road that ran close to the
railway, and as I was the bearer of the despatches and
obviously a ringleader of some sort, I was packed off
with a soldier at either side and a third man with a
drawn revolver behind. He was still smarting under my
abuse and he fired at my heel. The little soldier on my
left dropped his rifle, threw up his hands, and fell.
When I knelt beside him he was unconscious, and the
man with the revolver went into hysterics, rushed to
the other side of the road, and clutched his head and
wept. The third soldier went to console him, so, as it
was obvious that no one else would do anything practical for the unconscious man, I opened his tunic to
look for a wound. What I would do with it if I found it
was more than I had thought of, but at least I was better
qualified as a hospital orderly than my one-man medical
service, for he only shouted into the prostrate man's
ear what he thought was an Act of Contrition but was

really the Creed. I had my hand on the soldier's heart when he opened his eyes and said: "——ye all!" It was simple and final. Then he rose with great dignity, dusted himself, buttoned his tunic, shouldered his rifle, and resumed his march. Like myself he wasn't much of a soldier, but he had *savoir faire*.

I sat on the floor of the farmhouse parlour with several other prisoners—civilian truck drivers whose trucks had been commandeered for the campaign and were now standing outside in the farmyard. The woman of the house brought me dinner, but the look of the fat bacon made me sick. I wasn't a drinker, but just then I needed a drink badly, and the senior enemy officer, whose name seemed to be Mossie O'Brien, promised to buy me a flask of whisky at the first pub we passed. He had the same sort of good humour as Deasy, and I liked him as much as I disliked his truculent second-in-command.

At last his column, having collected all the local gossip, prepared to return into exile with their prizes; the engines of the trucks and cars were started, and I was actually being helped into one truck when a couple of shots rang out and we all dashed back to the farmhouse for cover. Our front-line troops had returned from Mass, indignant at what they regarded as a coward's blow, and the enemy were cut off from their base. At least I fervently hoped they were cut off. I was beginning to have my own doubts about our front line.

Back in the front room the enemy soldiers barricaded the little window with bags of meal and a can of pitch. The first blast of machine-gun fire from our Particularly Fierce Armoured Car knocked the pitch right over my driver's head. The realization that we had an armoured car at all depressed the defenders greatly. Except that it was top secret and had been withheld even from me, I should have told them that we had a Big Gun and nine shells as well. There were rifles stacked against the wall behind me, and several times I thought of grabbing one and turning it on the garrison—not because I was particularly brave but because I realized that they were even more scared than I was. At the same time, I knew that there was no help to be expected from my fellow prisoners. They were just saying their prayers. All I could do was to spread alarm and consternation before our men got cross and blew up the house. O'Brien came in and muttered to the other officer that a man had been killed upstairs, and I passed it on. I had to yell it at the deaf man who was reclining on my chest, and he shared my views of the gravity of the situation.

"Will we surrender now, Mossie?" he asked O'Brien, who was going out.

"Not till the last shot is fired," O'Brien said shortly.

"What did he say?" asked the deaf man.

"Not till the last shot is fired," I repeated with regret. I liked O'Brien, and I wished he wouldn't be quite so soldierly. I was tired of war and wanted to go home. I felt my first expedition into the heart of Ireland had brought me quite enough material to go on with. I knew that in Cork they would now be coming back down the Western Road after a walk along the river, and I longed to be there with Hendrick, telling him the story without waiting to see what might really happen. The deaf man too appeared to have an urgent engagement, because he began to unload his bandoleer into my coat pockets.

And after all the nonsense I had read about the excitement of one's baptism of fire, I was finding it intolerably dull. It just went on and on. The trucks and cars were still roaring in the farmyard, but one by one, as the petrol gave out or a bullet hit a petrol tank, they fell

silent like the instruments at the end of Haydn's "Farewell" symphony, and at last nothing was to be heard
but occasional bursts of fire. It drew on to evening, and
with the little window barricaded, we were almost in
darkness. The disagreeable officer was firing his revolver dispiritedly out the window and singing "You
Called Me Baby Doll a Year Ago" in a voice of agonizing
tunelessness. The deaf man fell asleep on my chest
and breathed nice and evenly at me through it all.

Then came a noise that woke even him, and then a
silence, and then a hysterical voice upstairs shouting
"Rifle grenade!" This was followed immediately by another voice shouting "Mossie is kilt!" and at once everyone began to wail "We surrender! We surrender!" Someone took out a large handkerchief and pushed it
through the window on a rifle barrel, but it went unnoticed and renewed fire filled them all with despair.
They were arguing about what they should do next
when I grabbed the handkerchief myself and ran out.
A soldier opened the door and closed it fast behind
me. I waved the handkerchief, but though shots continued to go off all round me there wasn't a soul to be
seen. Everything was blended in a rich, moss-green,
watery light, while from a mile away over the Limerick
grasslands came the distracted lowing of cows who had
gone unmilked and were sure the end of the world
was coming. The first man to climb the fence and approach the house was an old neighbour, Joe Ryan, but
the look on his long, pale face was that of a man drunk
with noise and tension, and I realized that I was in
great danger of being shot myself, through pure excitement. Once more heavy firing began from some distance away, and everyone bolted for cover, convinced
that it was all a trap. I had a terrible job persuading
both sides of the general good faith, all the time steer-

ing round behind me a group of prisoners who were in a highly nervous state and determined on regarding me as an old and intimate friend from whom they could not possibly be separated, and as proof of their affection they loaded me with rifles and bandoleers. Once I did have to intervene when a man with a drawn revolver attacked one of the prisoners whom he had recognized. As an example of the classic peripeteia soldiers after a surrender are remarkable: at one moment lords of the world dispensing life and death, at the next begging for their lives.

At the back of the house O'Brien, who had been shot through the mouth, was coughing up great gouts of blood while an old priest knelt beside him. Two soldiers brought downstairs the body of the young man who had been killed. He had been shot through the nostril, and the dried blood made a mocking third eye across his cheek, so that he might have been winking at us. Someone put a cap across his face; I saw that it was mine but I left it with him. I saw another civilian cap on the ground and I picked it up; caps cost money, and I knew if I came home without one I should hear about it from Father. It was only later that I realized I had picked up the dead boy's cap, which was drenched with blood. An old man and his daughter emerged from a cupboard under the stairs and asked: "Is it all over now, sir?"

Having seen the prisoners safe into Buttevant Barrack, I made my way home to Cork by the first car. I wanted to get my story into print, and, besides, I felt I had seen quite enough of the war for the time being. Nowadays I merely wonder at my own behaviour and remember with revulsion that I once wore a dead boy's blood-stained cap. It was not merely that I couldn't afford to lose a cap. I fancy the truth is that nothing of it was real to me, and it never once occurred to me that the boy whose cap I was wearing had that day been as living as myself, and perhaps loved his mother as much as I did mine. It was all as if I had read about it in *War and Peace*.

I doubt if most other people found it very real either. A few days later I accompanied Childers again to the "front," as I was now beginning to think of it. At Buttevant Barrack I met his cousin, David Robinson, who was in charge of the cavalry, such as it was. Robinson was another "damned Englishman," but of the sort I get along with. He was a typical British cavalry officer of the old school with a wide-brimmed hat, a coat that was old but elegant, well-cut riding breeches, and top-boots. He had a glass eye, a long, pale, beaky face, and the rather languid manner of a hard-boiled, soft-hearted gambler.

Childers wanted statements from our wounded, so he and I and a third man visited the Military Hospital, where, as usual, I disgraced myself, for inside the door with his head in bandages was a young enemy officer and I gave one startled look at him and then wrung his hands and said: "Mossie O'Brien!" I am, as I have said, a natural collaborationist, and O'Brien must have had the same weakness, for when he left hospital it was to join one of our columns. He was captured by his own side and sentenced to death, but escaped from the prison and lived to run a garage in his native town. On the other hand, my driver, for all his old guff about eating the despatches, was reported to have ended up on the other side. That was how things happened. What, after all, do you do when a well-established synthesis blows up on you but wonder whether you are really riding in the right compartment?

Childers also wanted to see the front line for himself. We had to walk along a road and across a railway bridge that was covered by enemy machine guns, and when I saw the officer in charge take cover and run I did the same, but Childers walked coolly across, studying the country and apparently unaware of danger. This, of course, was partly the attitude of the professional soldier who always knows by instinct when and where to take cover, but I felt there was also an element of absent-mindedness about it—the absent-mindedness of the old schoolmaster or parson who is so worried about what to do with Jones Minor's peculiar habits that he has no time to worry about himself. That night I watched him again in Ashill Towers, where the same country boys whose military genius I no longer had faith in occupied the upholstered chairs and studied their maps. There being no chair for Childers, nor anyone who valued his advice on military matters, he sat on a petrol can by the open door, his cap over his eyes and his mackintosh trailing on the floor, and went on scribbling his endless memoranda, articles and letters, like some old book-keeper who fears the new directors may think him superfluous. A tall, good-looking young American war correspondent who interviewed him on the petrol can congratulated him on Corkery's poem "Old Town of Gaelic Saint," which Hendrick and I had just published.

"Oh, yes," said Childers with a worried air, "but have you seen Mr. Brennan's poem—'Churchill Gave the Orders but England Gave the Guns'?" He always liked to keep conversation on a serious level.

My last experience of the front was when I was sent back to Buttevant Barrack to collect the Big Gun and the nine shells. The enemy had ensconced themselves in a substantial parsonage and could not be dislodged by rifle- and machine-gun fire. When I reached the barrack, the armourer, who had brought his beloved gun all the way from Dublin with him, was still working on the tenth shell and didn't want the gun fired till the shell was finished. But my orders were peremptory, and we loaded the little weapon and its shells on the back seat of my car. A mile or two from the parsonage we were intercepted by the officer in charge of the attack, and I was sent back to Buttevant with fresh instructions, so that I never really saw the weapon in action. Next day, however, I heard that after the first shell had been fired the enemy rushed out of the parsonage with their hands in the air, but, as in Kilmallock, this gesture had gone unnoticed. When the second shell sailed over their heads they came to the conclusion that they were to be massacred whether they surrendered or not, and took to their heels across the country. But this too went unobserved, and the whole nine shells were fired at the parsonage, without hitting it once.

I am not reporting what I saw, merely what I heard, but I do know that stranger things happened.

17

CHILDERS WAS at the front when Cork was attacked from the sea—a possibility our military geniuses had overlooked. Technically, a landing from the sea is supposed to be one of the most difficult of military operations, but as we handled the defence it was a walk-over. Hendrick and I had just got out our mimeographed news-sheet, describing the total defeat of the enemy; the newspaper boys were crying it through the streets, and Hendrick had fallen asleep on a pile of newsprint when I noticed the victors tearing through the city at forty miles an hour in the direction of the western highlands. We went to Headquarters at Union Quay to find out what we should say in our next number, but when we saw what was going on there we didn't even bother to enquire. There was a crowd of bewildered men in the roadway outside and a senior officer was waving his arms and shouting: "Every man for himself." We were both rather shaken. I was quite good on the Retreat from Moscow, but it looked as though the Retreat from Cork was going to be serious. Everybody was in a frenzy; it was no use asking for instructions or trying to bum a lift, so we locked up our office and set off on foot up the Western Road. Corkery had a little cottage in Inniscarra, five or six miles up the River Lee, where he was having a painting holiday, and we made up our minds to walk there and ask his advice. We never doubted but that he would know what to do in any emergency, literary, social, or military.

In spite of our bewilderment, it was an enchanting walk on a summer afternoon, climbing gently with the river till we passed the little abbey graveyard where my Grandfather O'Connor was buried, and we didn't mind the cars and lorries that tore past us literally in hundreds. Corkery favoured our pressing on to Macroom to find out if we were still wanted, and after he had given us a meal, we stood in the roadway with him, trying to halt one of the vehicles that went by. Childers was hanging frantically on the running board of one car, and he waved gaily to us as it passed. Naturally, nobody had thought of offering the "damned Englishman" his seat. Finally a truck came by at a crawl and it stopped at our signal and Corkery saw us aboard. When we had been travelling for a few minutes Hendrick suggested to the driver that he might put on a little more speed. It was only then we realized that we had got on to a lorry of explosives. Hendrick began to sing the poem O'Faolain had given us to print. It was to the tune of "John Brown's Body" and began: "In Clareside and in Kerryside we've buried fighting men." When he finished, the driver asked for another song, and I decided that our situation must be desperate indeed.

Neither Hendrick nor I had been in Macroom before, though it was the capital of the Irish-speaking west, but we got little chance of seeing what it was like because Corkery was there almost as soon as we were. Having seen us off, he had decided in his gentle, fatherly way that we were incapable of looking after ourselves, abandoned his painting holiday, and set off on our tracks. How he got a ride I don't know unless he actually shot one of the drivers, but there he was, and he dragged us back to Williams's Hotel, where he was staying. Childers was there as well. In the middle of the night some noisy men, pleading fatigue, began to hammer on our doors with rifle butts and demand our beds. We told them to go to Hell, but Childers got up at once and spent the rest of the night wandering about Macroom.

Next day the army was disbanded, all but special units like the engineers and ourselves. The staff had apparently realized that keeping an army in the field entailed too much work and had decided to revert to the sort of fighting it was accustomed to, sleeping in farmhouses, dropping down to the local pubs for a drink, and taking an occasional shot at a barrack or a lorry. The army was furious—naturally, since some of the poor devils were faced with an eighty-mile walk home—but Hendrick and myself, regarded as indispensable, felt complacent. David Robinson, who had retreated in excellent order from Ballincollig with horses and field kitchen, gave us lunch on the lawn before Macroom Castle. It was a queer party before the mediaeval castle with its crude Renaissance doorway; David Robinson putting everyone at his ease exactly as though he owned the place; members of the hungry disbanded army looking on; and exotic-looking women with queer accents arriving from Dublin with despatches warning us that the members of the Free State Government were determined on killing Childers. He was talking to Hendrick and me when one of them came up and said earnestly: "You know they will kill you if they catch you, Mr. Childers," and he turned away and said wearily: "Oh, why does everyone tell me that?" Robinson was the only one who took the reports seriously. He realized, as we didn't, that in a family row it is always the outsider who gets the blame. He took Hendrick and myself aside and asked if we would join him in hiring a fishing boat at Bantry and putting Childers ashore in France. France! To me it sounded like all the adventure stories of the world rolled into one, and even Hendrick, who made a point of not being demonstrative, looked enthusiastic. But we got a cold reception when we tried to explain Robinson's fears to members of the staff. "*Staff-Captain* Childers is under my command," said one of them, pulling rank on us, and though probably no one but Robinson suspected it, Childers's fate was decided that afternoon. The only man who could have saved him was De Valera, and he was somewhere in North Cork.

Instead, we commandeered a printing machine from the local job printers and had it carried to the schoolhouse at Ballymakeera, an Irish-speaking village in the mountains west of Macroom. To me, who had never seen the wilder parts of Ireland, Ballymakeera looked dry and cold, and the stones stuck up through the soil. Corkery, having seen us settled, went off to finish his painting holiday in the inn at Gougane Barra at the other side of the mountains. He had also probably asked a half-dozen people to keep an eye on us, though that didn't occur to me till I learned he had been hearing slanders about me. I don't deny that I may have given grounds for slander. It was the first time I had found myself in a purely Irish-speaking neighbourhood, and the phonetics went clean to my head. One day I sat for a full hour in the parlour of the little farmhouse, listening to a small boy outside playing numeral games and letting the sounds sink into my memory. My grandmother, of course, had spoken excellent Irish, but her teeth were not so good. I became very attached to the farmer, who also spoke excellent Irish and sometimes sat with me in the front room, talking or tapping out on his knee little rhymes he made up about me, like:

> *My son, Mick,*
> *My son, Mick,*
> *My son, Mick,*
>   *He is a fine man.*

As one can see they were not very good rhymes, but they were in good Irish, and, anyway, I can stand any number of rhymes in my own praise. I also fell in love with his elder daughter, whose gentle, blond, lethargic beauty was as breath-taking as her Irish, and she spoke that as I had never heard it spoken before, with style. Unfortunately, I had no notion of how to make love to her, because she appeared to me through a veil of characters from books I had read. Most of the time she was Maryanka from *The Cossacks*.

I loved everything else about that family—the warmth of the farmer, the cynicism of his wife, the wit and malice of the younger daughter, and the grave humour of the elder. Above all, I loved their perfect manners. They worked about three times as hard as anybody I had ever met, and Hendrick and I must have been pests, but they never showed it, and only afterwards when I learned to speak Irish properly did I realize what it must have cost them to listen to me speaking it.

But neither Tolstoy nor phonetics was in Childers's line at all. He asked petulantly why I went round as a walking arsenal (any fool could have told him I only did it to impress the girl I was in love with) and when his landlady would have her annual bath. He settled down with the printing press we had commandeered and went on with his articles and memoranda, and in his leisure hours sat under the apple tree in the schoolhouse garden and read *Deerslayer*. As I say, his literary standards were not high. One evening a couple of men burst in with the news that Michael Collins had been killed in an ambush near Bandon. I think they had the evening paper with them. Anyhow, they were rejoicing, and Hendrick and I rejoiced as well, and it was only later I remembered how Childers slunk away to his table silently, lit a cigarette, and wrote a leading article in praise of Collins. At the same time the newspapers continued to appear with bloodier stories of the fights and ambushes Childers himself was supposed to have led, and Hendrick and I only laughed at them. We, who didn't even know how to redraft and slant an agency message, couldn't be expected to understand how clever men prepare the way for someone's execution. Now, when I think of all the leads we got, I can only wonder all over again at our innocence.

At the same time, I fancy that Childers would have been very happy with a column to lead. I never for an instant saw under the weary, abstract superficies of a sick and unhappy man, but I could read, and I knew that Dumas and Fenimore Cooper meant a lot to him. One night when a raid was supposed to take place,

Childers got leave to join it—purely as an observer, of course—and worked himself into something that in an Englishman almost constituted a "state." There was a dance at the village hall, and the men stacked their rifles and danced "The Walls of Limerick" and "The Waves of Tory" before leaving for the battle. I couldn't dance, and the daughter of the house looked as though she might be busy for another hour, so I accompanied him back to the schoolhouse where the car was to pick him up. An American journalist went with us.

"Doesn't it remind you of Waterloo?" the American asked gently, referring to the noise of the dance hall behind us. " 'There was a sound of revelry by night' —you remember Byron?" Hendrick and I were not the only ones who worked at improving Childers's taste. Americans did it too, quite a lot, but it never seemed to have much effect on Childers.

"And you will remember the article on 'Women in the War,' won't you?" he asked anxiously. It wasn't a rebuke, but after all the years it comes back to me as a rebuke, to me rather than the American.

We left Childers at the schoolhouse, and he fell asleep over his trestle table. Nobody bothered to pick him up. After all, he was only a damned Englishman, elderly, sick, and absent-minded. Next time he got news of a raid, he took care to be on the spot, and as he unpinned his precious .22 from his braces, he gave Hendrick instructions about what to do with all his papers if he was killed. Next afternoon, Hendrick and I were sitting on the grass in the schoolhouse garden when he stepped out of a car, shrugging his shoulders disconsolately. "I'll never understand this country," he muttered. "I thought I was going off to a bloody combat, and instead, I found myself in Mick Sullivan's feather bed in Kilnamartyr."

233

The truth is that soldiering as Childers and Robinson understood it was too professional for our lads, who were amateurs to a man. It wasn't that they were less brave; it was simply that they had other things to attend to. Robinson decided to form a column and came to the schoolhouse one day to ask myself and Hendrick to join it, but once again we were blocked, and that was a great loss to literature, because during its brief existence, the column became a legend. Robinson was supposed to have planned one attack on the village of Inchigeela, in which, disguised as a tinker and carrying a baby, he would drive on an ass-cart to the barrack door, shoot the sentry, and hold the way open for his men. It was reported that before the engagement he addressed his troops, warning them that this would probably be the last time some of them would meet, and put such terror into them that they made at once for the hills, while Robinson, going from door to door, trying to borrow a baby, complained of the lack of patriotism in Irish mothers.

I find that difficult to believe, unless Robinson, with his dotty English sense of humour, was doing it as a joke, but there is certainly some truth in another story, for his column *did* capture the town of Kenmare, and then enemy reinforcements arrived and his troops took to their heels. Someone told me that the last he saw of Robinson was as he knelt in the middle of the Main Street, firing at the advancing troops and shouting over his shoulder in his English public-school drawl: "Come back, you Irish cowards!" All he would admit to me about that day in Kenmare was that, as a true British cavalry officer, he had made a boatload of men return under fire to pick up the last refugee from the battle. This turned out to be an Austrian Jew, who could barely speak English, but, finding himself unexpectedly in the middle of a battle, decided to make off with the silver. I need hardly say that Robinson was delighted with him and that the two became friends.

It was at this time that Corkery, deciding that I had seen enough of active service, ordered me home with him. Somebody had told him I was drinking, which was typical of Ireland, where a man can't have a private life, and, anyway, quite untrue, because drinking, like love-making and fighting, was something I still saw through a heavy veil of literature, and all the money Hendrick and I had was the remains of ten shillings we had borrowed from O'Faolain. Now if he had said I was going to hell with phonetics, I should have understood him at once. It was all no good. Corkery was convinced I was disgracing myself and Ireland, and home I must go. I remembered it later as the one occasion when I didn't want to go home, when I might almost have said like Faust to the flying moment: *"Verweile doch, du bist so schön!"*

Because of blown-up bridges, we had a long and wearisome ride home, getting out to let our car go across muddy fields, and we were finally dumped in a village miles from Cork. It was then I saw the Napoleon who was lost in Corkery, for he went straight to the house of a rich farmer, and, keeping his hand in his trouser pocket as though he had a gun, commandeered a pony and trap to take us the rest of the way to town.

After this, there was less fighting and less laughter. I slept away from home whenever I could find a bed, as much to escape Father as the enemy. News from the dear country I had left was bad. A whole edition of Childers's paper was thrown into a ditch because it had become too dangerous to transport. His printing press went over a mountain slope into a bog-

235

hole and could not be rescued. Finally, he set off with
Hendrick to headquarters and, since there was no further use for him, offered to remain and address enve-
lopes. He was told—rather tactlessly, I thought—that
he was a much-wanted man, and his presence was a
danger to others.

So he and Robinson set out on a fantastic journey
across Ireland, sleeping by day and travelling by night.
I hope there is some record of it among his papers, for
as Robinson told it to me years later in his light, mocking English way it was like a long section from one of
the nineteenth-century adventure stories that Childers
loved. One night in North Cork, Robinson, who was
cycling beside Childers, skidded into a ditch and broke
his shoulder bone. When he came to his senses he was
in a country cottage and a crowd of people were shouting: "Take him away! Take him away!" for by this
time the two damned Englishmen had become the
most unwelcome guests in Ireland. They found shelter
in the home of Liam Lynch, and, when Robinson's
shoulder had healed, resumed their night journeys.
Tipperary was so crammed with troops searching for
them that they had to cross Slievenamon mountain by
night, and in the darkness they tramped up a dry wa-
tercourse where a single slip meant death. Dawn was
breaking as they got near the top, and there, in the
doorway of a cottage, stood a local gallant armed to the
teeth, while on the plain beneath them three columns
of infantry converged on the mountain. "Ah, don't be
afraid," the local hero told them. " 'Tis me they're after.
I went into three towns, and in every town I left a message to tell them where they'd find me."

Thinking this cottage unsafe, the two hunted men
plunged down through a mountain mist to a second
cottage, and there they discovered a second national

hero in full uniform lying on a sofa while two pretty girls fed him chocolate creams. They finally reached the house of their cousin, Robert Barton—another British officer—in County Wicklow, and were captured there through the treachery of one of Barton's servants. They were given adjoining cells, between which some earlier prisoner had dug a tiny hole. They were both passionate chess-players, so they chalked chessboards on the floor, made chessmen out of newspapers, and played until the morning when Childers went out to die before an Irish firing squad. Robinson's premonitions that afternoon in front of Macroom Castle had been finally justified. The only charge against Childers was the possession of arms—the little toy pistol I had taken from him that day outside the English Market and which he was trying to unpin from his braces when the soldiers grabbed him.

I was in a house on the Wellington Road the morning I read of his execution, and I wrote the date over Whitman's lines on the death of Lincoln in the copy of *Leaves of Grass* that I always carried with me at the time—"Hushed Be the Camps Today." Like everything else I did at the time, it reeked of literature, and yet when I recite the lines to myself today, all the emotion comes back and I know it was not all literature. As I say, I am a collaborationist, and Childers was one of the very few people I have met with whom I had no communication of any sort: if, as I hope, his papers of the time have survived, I know that I must appear in them as a sort of Handy Andy, described completely from outside, for there is nothing in nature more removed from the imaginative boy than the grown man who has cut himself apart from life, seems to move entirely by his own inner light, and to face his doom almost with equanimity. And yet again and again in my own imagination, I have had to go through those last few terrible moments with him almost as though I were there: see the slight figure of the little grey-haired Englishman emerge for the last time into the Irish daylight, apparently cheerful and confident but incapable of grandiose gestures, concerned only lest inadvertently he might do or say something that would distress some poor fool of an Irish boy who was about to level an English rifle at his heart.

18

THE PERIOD FROM the end of 1922 to the spring of 1923 was one that I found almost unbearably painful. I still had no money nor any way of earning it. Sometimes I slept in the house of Sean French, who was in prison; sometimes I went off with a friend whom I shall call Joe Clery and his friend, and the three of us spent the night in a hay-barn or commandeered beds for ourselves in a big house on Montenotte. Clery and his friend fascinated me. Both were swift, cool, and resourceful, and seemed to enjoy the atmosphere of danger as much as I dreaded it. Corkery, with whom I discussed them, suggested that the Russian Revolution had shown that after a certain stage, control of a revolutionary movement passes from the original dreamers to men who are professional revolutionaries.

I am afraid that Corkery saw historical prototypes as I saw literary ones, and that there was more than that to it. The romantic improvisation was tearing right down the middle, and on both sides the real killers were emerging. One morning Clery told me that we were needed for a "job" that evening. The "job" was to shoot unarmed soldiers courting their girls in deserted laneways, and the girls as well if there was any danger of our being recognized. I lost my head, and said I would put a stop to the "job" in one way if I couldn't do it in another. Clery felt as I did and agreed that I should consult Corkery, who was my authority for everything. It was hard luck on Corkery, but he accepted this as he accepted every other responsibility, and advised me to see Mary MacSwiney, Terence's sister and our local representative in Parliament. I went to her house and she received me very coldly. She thought me an indiscreet young man, which, indeed, I was. "You seem to have some moral objection to killing women," she said disapprovingly, and when I admitted that I had, she added complacently; "I see no *moral* objection, though there may be a *political* one." I stayed in her house till a messenger returned from the local commandant to say that the operation had been called off.

It was clear to me that we were all going mad, and yet I could see no way out. The imagination seems to paralyse not only the critical faculty but the ability to act upon the most ordinary instinct of self-preservation. I could be obstinate enough when it came to the killing of unarmed soldiers and girls because this was a basic violation of the imaginative concept of life, whether in the boys' weeklies or the Irish sagas, but I could not detach myself from the political attitudes that gave rise to it. I was too completely identified with them, and to have abandoned them would have meant abandoning faith in myself.

Any moments of relaxation and sanity that came to me were in the few houses I visited, like the Barrys' in Windsor Cottages, the O'Learys' on Gardiner's Hill, or the Frenches' on the Wellington Road. The French household consisted of his mother and four sisters. Kitty O'Leary, Hendrick's girl, was a great friend of the family, and when she called, the four sisters mustered about her at the piano and sang all the music-hall songs of the time—"Oh, It's a Windy Night Tonight," "Sally, Sally!" and "I Left My Love in Avalon" while I listened with the emotions of a seminarist at a ribald party. As a reward, at the end of the evening Kitty played a Schubert Fantasia and sang a couple of seventeenth-century *bergerettes*—"*Maman, dites-moi*" and "*Non, je n'irai plus au bois.*" At ten precisely, Mrs. French, who looked and talked like someone out of a Jane Austen novel, asked what I should like to drink, and the "girls" ranged themselves behind her and laid one finger flat on the top of another to indicate that I must ask for tea. Otherwise they would have to drink hot milk! All those homes were matriarchies. It is an Ireland that is disappearing, an Ireland arranged for the convenience of some particular man, where women—some of whom were more brilliant than any man in the household and risked their lives just as much—worked harder than servant girls and will probably never realize why it is that when I look back on the period, it is of them rather than of their brothers that I think. In those days, when the French girls had drunk their hard-earned cup of tea and gone to bed, and lorries of soldiers tore up the city hills on their sinister errands, I merely read Whitman or hummed:

> *Je connais trop le danger*
> *Ou l'amour pourrait m'engager.*

That was a danger that wouldn't really engage me for a good many years, and meanwhile I had other dangers to think of. I was captured effortlessly one spring morning by two Free State soldiers. Fortunately for myself I didn't have a gun. They marched me to their headquarters in the Courthouse.

Imprisonment came as a relief because it took all responsibility out of my hands, and, as active fighting died down and the possibility of being shot in some reprisal execution diminished, it became—what else sums up the period so well?—a real blessing. Not, God knows, that the Women's Gaol in Sunday's Well was anything but a nightmare. The first night I spent there after being taken from the Courthouse I was wakened by the officer of the watch going his round. As he flashed his torch about the cell he told us joyously that there had been a raid on the house of Michael Collins's sister in Blarney Lane and one of the attackers had been captured with a revolver and would be executed. (How was I to know that the irony of circumstances would make me the guest of Michael Collins's sister in that very house before many years had passed?) I fell asleep again, thinking merely that I was very fortunate to be out of the Courthouse where the soldiers would probably have taken it out on me. Towards dawn I was wakened by the tall, bitter-tongued man I knew as "Mac," and I followed him down the corridor. A Free State officer was standing by the door of one cell, and we went in. Under the window in the gas-light that leaked in from the corridor what seemed to be a bundle of rags was trying to raise itself from the floor. I reached out my hand and shuddered because the hand that took mine was like a lump of dough. When I saw the face of the man whose hand I had taken, I felt sick, because that was also like a lump of dough. "So that's how you treat your prisoners?" Mac snarled at the officer. Mac, like my father, was an ex-British soldier, and had the old-fashioned attitude that you did not strike a defenceless man. The officer, who in private life was probably a milkman, began some muttered rigmarole about the prisoner's having tried to burn a widow's home and poured petrol over the sleeping children. "Look at that!" Mac snarled at me, paying no attention to him. "Skewered through the ass with bayonets!" I waited and walked with the boy to the head of the iron stairs where the suicide net had been stretched to catch any poor soul who found life too hard, and I watched him stagger painfully down in the gas-light. There were only a half-dozen of us there, and we stood and watched the dawn break over the city through the high unglazed windows. A few days later the boy was shot. That scene haunted me for years—partly, I suppose, because it was still uncertain whether or not I should be next, a matter that gives one a personal interest in any execution; partly because of the overdeveloped sense of pity that had made me always take the part of kids younger or weaker than myself; mainly because I was beginning to think that this was all our romanticism came to—a miserable attempt to burn a widow's house, the rifle butts and bayonets of hysterical soldiers, a poor woman of the lanes kneeling in some city church and appealing to a God who could not listen, and then—a barrack wall with some smug humbug of a priest muttering pray-

243

ers. (I heard him the following Sunday give a sermon on the dangers of company-keeping.) I had been able to think of the Kilmallock skirmish as though it was something I had read of in a book, but the battered face of that boy was something that wasn't in any book, and even ten years later, when I was sitting reading in my flat in Dublin, the door would suddenly open and he would walk in and the book would fall from my hands. Certainly, that night changed something for ever in me.

But I was young, and somehow or other I had to go on living, even in that dreadful place. There were four of us in a cell that had been condemned as inadequate for one, and the one who had originally occupied it had done so in an age when they didn't believe in coddling prisoners. It was seething with vermin. Three of us slept on the floor with our heels to the door and one on the radiator pipes under the window, and that took in the total floor space. My cell-mates were not exactly the type I had been accustomed to, and how ninety per cent of the men in prison had got there at all was beyond me. Cremin was the only one of my cell-mates that I could talk to. He was an ex-British army man with a cruel wound in the belly he had got from the Germans in the First World War. By day he made rings out of shilling pieces impaled on an iron spike while I read *Hermann und Dorothea:* at night, when the other men were kneeling and saying the rosary about the suicide net, he and I sang songs against one another.

The *Hermann und Dorothea* had, of course, come from Corkery, who signed himself "Martin Cloyne," feeling sure that no one on the enemy side would ever have read his novel or recognized the name of its hero. He complained amusingly of a visit from Clery and his friend, and his sister's discovery of the remains of a half-dozen of stout behind his bookcase—"These secret, midnight revels, and we in our most innocent slumber!" With the book had come a box of Three Castles cigarettes. Heine, he added, was the proper poet for a man in prison, "but this, being only a university town, has never heard of Heine." Characteristically, after this, he sent me tobacco and cigarette papers, because, as he said, it might be good for my character to have to roll my own cigarettes. How well that gentle little man understood me!

I replied in the only language I understood. The Women's Prison overlooked the Women's Penitentiary run by the Good Shepherd nuns, and when the penitents walked in the garden in their starched white linen coifs, the prisoners crowded to the tall window recesses and whistled at them through the bars. Someone beside myself was shocked, for after the Rosary on that first night, a small, black, bitter man made an impassioned protest, and I wrote to Corkery to say that the first person I had noticed in gaol was Baburin, the hero of Turgenev's great story. I was still at the stage of seeing Turgenev and Dostoevsky characters everywhere. It was a little closer to reality than Cu Chulainn and Werther, but not much.

Early one morning we were driven through the city to Glanmire Station, and after a long wait in the place where I had already endured so much, we were locked in old-fashioned carriages and the train set off. As it emerged from the tunnel at Rathpeacon we all rushed to the windows to catch a final glimpse of Cork. At Mallow the viaduct was blown up (Childers was supposed to have done it), so we were marched through the town to the railway station. It was April and the whole country looked lovely.

We were locked in our carriages again with nothing but tinned fish to eat, and when the others developed a thirst they could not quench, I was glad I had not been able to eat it. It was dark when we reached Dublin, and after another long halt, we were shunted across the city to Amiens Street and off into the countryside again. The sea was on our right-hand side. None of us knew this part of the country, and we had no notion of where we were going. The Free State Government had been negotiating with the British Government for the renting of St. Helena to use as a prison, and the general impression was that we were going there. Instead, we stopped at a wayside station in flat pastoral country about an hour's run from Dublin. In the distance a searchlight moved petulantly up and down the sky and over the fields, picking out white-washed cottages and trees in their first leaf and flattening them against the night like pieces of theatre scenery. We marched towards the searchlight, and it flicked along with us, half human in its mechanical precision, till it became a new sensation like hunger and weariness, and gave everything a hallucinatory look.

At last a group of low, irregular buildings emerged, changing continuously like the images in a kaleidoscope—a long whitewashed hall, a group of dark wooden huts with every board defined by shadow as if by blown snow, a tall gate set in a high fence of barbed wire and lit by arc-lamps. Outside this was another row of wooden huts that seemed to serve as offices and in front of these we were left standing for hours in the cold as the prisoners were checked in, a half-dozen at a time. It was early morning when I was escorted through the main gate. At the quartermaster's store I was given a spring bed, a mattress, blankets, and tinware, but when I tried to carry them I fainted. A military policeman helped me to my hut and showed me how to fix my bed, while other prisoners called from their beds to enquire where I had come from and who was with me. All were looking for their own friends and relatives.

Next morning, when I opened my eyes in a real bed, and a man leaving the hut let in a breath of morning air and a glimpse of green fields and blue sky, I felt I was dreaming. That is what I think of whenever I hear the Good Friday music from *Parsifal:*

> *Doch sah ich nie so mild und zart*
> *Die Halmen, Blüthen und Blumen.*

It was a long, high, well-lit hut, divided down the middle by a wooden partition that was about as high as a man, and at either side of it and along the walls were rows of beds, metal beds, and wooden beds made of three boards, twenty-five or thirty beds in a row, and all the men were still asleep, wrapped in their brown military blankets. My own bed was against a wall beside a window, and through the window I could see another hut of the same kind across the way. A whistle blew from outside and the little man who had blown it entered the hut and came down between the two rows of beds. When he reached mine and saw me awake, he stopped and instead of blowing on his police whistle he whistled "Kelly the Boy from Killan," at the same time marking time and miming an elaborate conversation in which he discussed with me the slothfulness of the younger generation, the beauty of the morning, and the delight of one gentleman on meeting another, which was apparently his idea of a joke. I replied in the same way—that morning I was in the mood for seeing jokes—and he raised his hat to march time and went on, blasting away again at his police whistle.

Later came more whistles, and the men dressed hastily and made their beds. Military policemen stationed themselves outside each hut and we stood at ease at the foot of our beds. Another whistle blew outside the door, the hut-leader gave an order, and the men sprang to attention. Then a military officer, accompanied by one of our own staff, entered and passed quickly between the rows of beds, both counting. Nominally we stood to attention only for our own officer. This was part of the camp organization, and I began by admiring it greatly. It duplicated completely the enemy organization so that none of our men ever made contact with their gaolers. Our quartermaster indented for supplies to the enemy quartermaster; our postmaster received our mail from the enemy postmaster; we stood to attention to be counted by our own officer. It was all very dignified and practical. Or so I thought.

Count, because of the new arrivals, dragged intolerably that morning, and after it came Mass, which was attended only by a handful of men. It was held in the big dining hall, and only the acolyte, a pacifist by conviction, was permitted to communicate. We who were not were not allowed to receive the sacraments. After Mass the whistle blew for breakfast, and I collected my knife, fork, spoon, mug, and plate and found my way back to the dining hall. It struck me that the life was going to suit me fine. Within an hour or two I was roped into the teaching staff to teach Irish, for there were an almost unlimited number of students but hardly any teachers. The classes, consisting only of men who attended because they wanted to learn, were excellent, and the teaching standard was high.

Spanish was taught by Fred Cogley, who had spent a lot of his life in South America, French by his son. The two of them shared a room with Childers's friend, Frank Gallagher. It was a joy to sit and talk with them and feel that I was back with the sort of people who had really started the Revolution—men who read books and discussed general ideas. They were the type I had looked up to for years and I like looking up to people; it gives me a sense of direction.

All I needed now was to rid myself of the lice I had brought from that foul gaol. Fortunately the weather was fine, and I could wash my clothes and air them in the grass. Besides, the camp was an American aerodrome, dating from the First World War; the American plumbing still functioned spasmodically, and each morning I rose before anyone else was awake, took a cold shower and a brisk walk of a couple of miles round the compound, and prepared my lessons before Mass, and each morning the nightmare of the Civil War grew fainter in my mind, the sleepless nights, the aimless skirmishes, and the futile, sickening executions. I loved that early-morning freedom, with the rich fields of Meath all round me and the possibility of silence and recollection before the others came awake, because for the rest of the day the big hut was full of noise and movement, wrestling matches and arguments. Some of the men hammered away at rings, others stood at the partition and wove macrame bags, and there was a continuous coming and going of people mad with boredom, restless, inquisitive, and talkative. Now it was a Clare officer with a nervous temperament who wanted to discuss the immortality of the soul, now a West of Ireland teacher who dreamed of becoming a great lawyer and would smile and cry: "Ah, to be able to sway vast crowds by the magic of

the human voice!" The French Grammar I was studying would be sufficient in itself to halt half a dozen
visitors, some with mothers who had spoken French
like natives, others who had not availed themselves of
the chance of studying it at school and would regret
it till their dying day. Anything for the chance of a
conversation! It had its advantages, of course, for one's
mind was always exposed to the play of new impressions, but it left one crazy for privacy.

The camp was quiet again only on fine afternoons
when a majority of the men marched out to the rec-
reation field to play football or watch it. Sometimes I
went with them for the sake of the view across the
fields to the sea, just to recite to myself: "It keeps
eternal whisperings around desolate shores," but usually I found it pleasanter to remain behind and work.
Apart from the lack of privacy, boredom was the great
curse and routine its only alleviation; this was what
was so good about the military organization of the
camp.

A serious gap in my education was revealed to me
during the very first days when I prepared my lessons
for class, and the shock nearly killed me. I opened an
Irish Grammar for what must have been the first time
and read it through with a sinking heart. M. Jourdain's
astonishment on discovering that he had been talking
prose all his life was nothing to mine on discovering
that I had been talking grammar—and bad grammar
at that. Even my training as a teacher had been mainly
confined to texts and conversation. I don't mean that I
hadn't heard of nouns, verbs, and adjectives, because
obviously I could have learned nothing if I hadn't
learned that, but I had not taken it seriously. For me,
languages had always been a form of magic, like girls,
and I would as soon have thought of taking liberties

with one as with the other. Now I started reciting to myself from my little hoard of Irish and German poetry, realizing that if the poet used one form of a word instead of another, it was not because he liked it better but because it was the correct one.

Whatever the importance of grammar in reading or writing, as an image of human life it seems to me out on its own. I have never since had any patience with the apostles of usage. Usage needs no advocates, since it goes on whether one approves of it or not, and in doing so breaks down the best-regulated languages. Grammar is the bread-winner of language as usage is the housekeeper, and the poor man's efforts at keeping order are for ever being thwarted by his wife's intrigues and her perpetual warnings to the children not to tell Father. But language, like life, is impossible without a father and he is forever returning to his thankless job of restoring authority. As an emotional young man, I found it a real help to learn that there was such a thing as an object, whether or not philosophers admitted its existence, and that I could use the accusative case to point it out as I would point out a man in the street. In later years George Moore fell in love with the subjunctive—a pretty little mood enough, though, as his books show, much too flighty for a settled man.

Maybe it was the grammar that started me off, or maybe the grammar itself was only a symptom of the emergence from a protracted adolescence, but I was beginning to have grave doubts about many of the political ideas I had held as gospel. One was that the Irish Republic founded in 1916 still existed, that it could not be disestablished except by the free choice of the people—free choice being one exercised in the complete absence of external compulsion; that the shadow government that accepted its principles was the only lawful one and that we could not sit in a usurping parliament. I began to see that the form of choice that was postulated was a rather ideal one, and said that the idea of abstaining from attendance in parliament was absurd. Only one of my new acquaintances agreed with me. He was Tom Walsh, an Irish-speaker from Clare who, when he met me, remembered a poem I had published in some political weekly. It is only in the wilder parts of Ireland, where a newspaper is an event, that a studious, lonely young farmer would remember a poem like that. Walsh was powerfully built; he shambled about with his head down, a lock of dark hair dangling over one eye and with a vague, shy air as though he hoped you would be kind enough not to notice him. But his big features had a shimmering delicacy that revealed an inner conflict; he had a slight stammer that exaggerated his slowness of speech, and when he was at his most earnest there appeared on each temple a slight pallor as though with him thought were something physical, like lifting a great weight. His smile, usually wistful, but sometimes joyous and mischievous, was like sunlight over a western moor. I knew he wrote poetry in Irish but he wouldn't show it to me, and when I pressed him about it, he only became distressed. His diffidence must have run in the family, for he once described to me how his father had caught the local thief at their potato pit by night, and, frenzied with embarrassment at seeing a neighbour do wrong, could only wave his arms and cry: "Ah, what will the soul do at the Judgement?" (What the thief said the soul would do was very coarse but probably accurate.)

Walsh was even more disturbed than I was about our political affiliations. His eyebrows would go up into his limp dark hair, and the two white spots would show on either temple as he stammered: "I believe the bishops are right to excommunicate us. If I was a bishop I'd do the same."

"Then what are you doing here?" I would ask, and Walsh would throw back his head and laugh softly and secretly at the absurdity of his position. To me it was no laughing matter. I knew that a countryman like Walsh was always slightly abashed before abstract ideas, but if I once convinced myself that the other side was in the right, I should never rest until I had made my position plain. I am sure we were both held back by our admiration for the majority of those among whom we had been thrown. We had our share of fatheads in the camp, and maybe a crook or two, but on an average the prisoners were far finer types than either of us would have met in a normal lifetime in Ireland—better educated, more unselfish, thoughtful, and interesting; and though it is all close on forty years ago I still find myself thinking of men I knew there and wondering what life has made of them and they of life. Walsh and I used to study the autograph albums that were always circulating in the camp to see what there was in the quotations to account for our uneasiness. We noticed a preponderance of quotations from Shelley and his followers, like Meredith, with his:

Our life is but a little holding lent
  To do a mighty labour; we are one
With Heaven and the stars when it is spent
  To serve God's aim—else die we with the sun!

It wasn't that I didn't admire Meredith, but in quotations like that there was altogether too much about dying for my taste, and it wasn't even the harmless, sugary nineteenth-century dying of Tennyson or

Christina Rossetti that always moved me to tears. This
was dying for its own sweet sake, and I began to wonder if there was not some relationship between Irish
nationalism and the Romantic movement. Gallagher
was the great Shelleyan of the camp, and after I had
listened to him lecture on Erskine Childers, I complained to him that there wasn't a single characteristic touch of Childers in it. One evening I sat in the
hut and listened to a Corkman singing in a little group
about some hero who had died for Ireland and the
brave things he had said and the fine things he had
done, and I listened because I liked these simple little
local songs that continued to be written to the old
beautiful ballad airs and that sometimes had charming verses, like:

I met Pat Hanley's mother and she to me did say,
"God be with my son Pat, he was shot in the runaway;
"If I could kiss his pale cold lips his wounded heart I'd
*   cure*
"And I'd bring my darling safely home from the valley
*   of Knockanure."*

But half-way through this song I realized that it
was about the boy whose hand I had taken in the
Women's Prison in Cork one morning that spring, and
suddenly the whole nightmare came back. "It's as well
for you fellows that you didn't see that lad's face when
the Free Staters had finished with it," I said angrily.
I think it must have been that evening that the big
row blew up, and I had half the hut shouting at me.
I shouted as well that I was sick to death of the worship
of martyrdom, that the only martyr I had come close to
was a poor boy from the lanes like myself, and he
hadn't wanted to die any more than I did; that he had
merely been trapped by his own ignorance and sim-

plicity into a position from which he couldn't escape, and I thought most martyrs were the same. "And Pearse?" somebody kept on crying. "What about Pearse? I suppose he didn't want to die either?" "Of course he didn't want to die," I said. "He woke up too late, that was all." And that did really drive some of the men to fury.

I went to bed myself in a blind rage. Apparently the only proof one had of being alive was one's readiness to die as soon as possible: dead was the great thing to be, and there was nothing to be said in favour of living except the innumerable possibilities it presented of dying in style. I didn't want to die. I wanted to live, to read, to hear music, and to bring my mother to all the places that neither of us had ever seen, and I felt these things were more important than any martyrdom. After that, whenever I saw a quotation from Shelley or one of his followers in an autograph album, I usually inserted a line or two of Goethe as near as possible to it. My favourite was: "One must be either the hammer or the anvil."

And in spite of all the sentimental high-mindedness, I felt it went side by side with an extraordinary inhumanity. Or maybe angularity is the better word. It was really the lack of humour that seems to accompany every imaginative improvisation, and in other ways I must have been as humourless as everybody else.

The first incident that revealed to me what the situation was really like was funny enough. A man, whose name was, I think, Frank Murphy, had had a disagreement with his hut-leader about the amount of fatigues he had to do, so he refused to do any more. There was nothing unusual about this, of course. In an atmosphere where there was no such thing as privacy and people were always getting on one another's nerves, it was inevitable, and the sensible thing would have been to transfer Murphy to another hut. But this was against our principles. We had a complete military organization that duplicated and superseded that of our gaolers, and any slight on this was a slight on the whole fiction it was based on. Murphy was summoned before a court martial of three senior officers, found guilty, and sentenced to more fatigues. Being a man of great character, he refused to do these as well. This might have seemed a complete stalemate, but not to imaginative men. The camp command took over from the enemy a small time-keeper's hut with barred windows to use as a prison, and two prisoners, wearing tricolour armlets to show that they really were policemen and not prisoners like the rest of us, arrested Murphy and locked him up. That night Walsh and I, who both liked Murphy, visited him in his prison and talked to him through the bars of his window, while I looked round me at the tall sentry posts and beneath them the camp command taking its regular evening walk as prisoners of the men in the sentry posts, while *their* prisoner stared at them through the bars of his window and talked bitterly of justice and injustice. I felt the imaginative improvisation could not go farther than that, but it did. Murphy still had a shot in his locker, for he went on hunger strike, not against our gaolers but his own, and—unlike them when they went on hunger strike soon after—he meant it.

This was too much even for men who affected to believe that the Irish Republic was still in existence and would remain so, no matter what its citizens might think, so a mass meeting was held in the dining hall, and the various officers addressed us on the wickedness of Murphy's defiance of majority rule. From people who were in prison for refusing to recognize majority rule and who had even been excommunicated for it, this was pretty thick. When it was proposed to release Murphy and boycott him, and all those in favour were asked to raise their hands, nine hundred odd hands were raised. When those against were called on, one hand went up, and that was mine. Later in life I realized that it was probably the first time I had ever taken an unpopular stand without allies.

ALL THE SAME, that summer was exceedingly
happy. When the weather was fine, I held
my classes on the grass outside some hut. In fact,
since Father had gone to the War in 1914 I had never
been so well off. I was still only nineteen; thanks to the
American plumbing, I lived a healthier life than I
could have lived at home; I had regular and pleasant
work to do—I was now teaching German as well as
Advanced Irish—and I knew I was doing it well. For
me, who had lived all my life by faith, it was an ex-
hilarating experience to know that I was doing something well by objective standards. Above all, I had
friends I liked and admired. Apart from Walsh, there
was Cathal Buckley, the youngest of us, who had a fat,
pale, schoolboy face and a quiet clerical manner, and

Ned Moriarty from Tralee, a British ex-soldier, who was tall, thin, and Spanish-looking and whose hands were more expressive than other people's faces. Apart from these, my immediate friends, there were others from whom I learned a lot like Gallagher, Cogley, Sean T. O'Kelly (later President) who lent me Anatole France in French, and Sean MacEntee (later Minister for Finance), who gave me the Heine I had coveted so long and proved that Corkery was right and that Heine *was* the proper poet for a man in prison.

But there was no lack of interesting people. There was the quartermaster, for instance. He was a North Corkman, small and thin, with a thin, desperate face, burning blue eyes, and a tiny mustache which he tugged as though the tugging provided all the energy he needed. He needed plenty, because he seemed to go by clockwork, swinging his arms wider than anyone else, and he had a capacity for swearing and bad language that beat anything I ever heard. All the North Corkmen swore well, but he swore artistically, so that you immediately forgot whatever he was swearing about and merely admired the skill with which he did it. And after he had cursed you through every byway of his fancy, he would grab you by the collar and mutter: "That suit is in rags! Bloody fellow that can't even look after himself! Come over to the store till I make you look decent!" I think he had a sneaking regard for me too, for he once told me I might become a great man myself if only I imitated a certain politician in the camp who practised oratory before the mirror every day. "And I once heard him give a lecture on Robert Emmett before a thousand people and there wasn't one that wasn't sobbing. That's what you should do!"

In fact, it was the nearest thing I could have found

to life on a college campus, the only one I was really fitted for, and I should have been perfectly happy except that I was still doing it at my mother's expense. It was all very well to be teaching German and Irish, but I still had no clothes and no boots except what I got from the quartermaster's store, and the overcoat I used as an extra blanket was an old belted blue coat with a fur collar that somebody who was throwing it away gave to Mother. It looked absurd on me, but it was the only warm thing I had. I knew what those weekly parcels from her cost—the cake, the tin of cocoa, the tin of condensed milk, and the box of cigarettes—and I felt sure that she was going out to daily work to earn them for me. That was true. One day one of the soldiers, who had served with Father in the old Munster Fusiliers, got himself transferred to the garbage collection and brought me a letter from her. She had got work in the house of a plumber on Summerhill who was supposed to have "influence" and would try to get me released. In an emotional fit I replied that when I got out I would not be a burden to her for long, and she replied in a sentence that I knew did not apply particularly to me and was merely part of her attitude to life—"If there were no wild boys there would be no great men."

But towards the end of the year things began to go to hell. Fighting outside had definitely ended; De Valera had issued a cease-fire order but had refused either to surrender or negotiate (the Government of the Irish Republic, being the only lawful one, could not possibly negotiate with impostors), and we were left to play football and study Irish behind barbed wire. The Free State Government was incapable of letting the prisoners go as a generous gesture. But all the same, people were being released, in ones and twos

260

and on no basis that anybody could understand, so that it became harder to concentrate and plan. Classwork had suddenly become very difficult, and the certificates I signed for successful students had an air of finality about them.

Then one day a disciple of Gallagher's called Joe Kennedy and myself heard that a group of prisoners who had made themselves objectionable had been evicted from their room in the Limerick hut. We were both studious and suffered greatly from the noise in the bigger huts. The Limerick men, when we went to interview them, turned out to be a splendid crowd, and they urged us to come in with them. We applied and got the room.

Only after we had done so did we realize that we had committed the unforgivable sin. If we had not applied, no one else would have done it, and in a couple of days the original occupants would have crept quietly back. That is how things happen in Ireland. We were in the middle of a land war, and we were grabbers too proud to withdraw. I coveted that room almost to the point of insanity. I wanted a place to myself where I could go and read. I had written an essay on Turgenev which I had submitted to a national competition, and for some reason now known only to God, I was translating *Lorna Doone* into Irish. I had never seen the book before, and have never looked at it since, so I cannot even guess what attraction it had for me.

Walsh helped us to carry our beds and mattresses into the new hut under a fire of taunts and threats from the dispossessed and their friends, and Kennedy, a tall, handsome man, with a long, bony shaven skull and a squint, turned and denounced them in a cavernous voice that made me think of Savonarola. That should have been sufficient warning to me, because I am sure that Savonarola and I would never have got on under the one roof. The Limerick men dropped in to make us feel at home and they and I became fast friends. They were a curious lot, quite different from any other county group I had met in the camp, independent and apparently indifferent to what anybody thought of them. This was curious, for Limerick has always been a hot-bed of fanaticism, the only place in Ireland to tolerate anti-Semitic riots. I can only suppose that after the public opinion of Limerick, any other seemed a joke.

The arrangement worked excellently as far as they and I were concerned. They were the only group who sang in harmony, and I had a passion for part-singing though I didn't know enough about music to join in it. Every night we met in their big room and brewed our tea and cocoa, and I got them to sing, and they dragged me into arguments. Here again, they were different from all the other groups, for though they shouted and gibed and laid down the law, they didn't seem to resent my heresies in the least. But Kennedy did. He was chock-full of mystical nationalism which I found much more exasperating than mystical religion, though I often felt they were the same thing: the only difference was that along with an invisible God who was the fourth wall of our earthly stage the mystics wanted an invisible Ireland as well. Living in the presence of God was one thing; living in the presence of Ireland was more than I could tolerate. Kennedy began to sound more and more like Savonarola, and soon our cozy, quiet little room no longer attracted me. I know now that the fault was mine, because I was young and desperately trying to think things out for myself for the first time. Soon we were barely talking, and he made a public profession of faith by pinning over his bed a manuscript poem of Gallagher's with the stock reference to martyrdom—"Death's iron discipline," if my memory of it is right. With youthful contentiousness I wrote out over my own bed my favourite lines from *Faust—Grau, teurer Freund . . .* ('Grey, my dear friend, is all your theory and green the golden tree of Life'). The word "Life" seemed to affect Kennedy as the word "Death" affected me, and he accused me of "beastly, degrading cynicism" and took off his coat to fight me. After that we didn't speak again till the tragi-comedy ended in the national hunger strike, and he took up his bed and returned to a hut where he could endure "Death's iron discipline" among loyal comrades. Fortunately, he thought better of it and lived to be a distinguished parliamentarian of whom I could say complacently: "Yes, he and I were in gaol together," which is rather like the English "He and I were in Eton together" but considerably more classy.

At the same time an incident occurred that probably made me more intolerant than I might otherwise have been. The Free State authorities gave parole as the Catholic Church gave the sacraments—in return for a signed declaration that one would behave oneself for the future, and opinion in the camp was dead against this, though, in fact, there was no fighting and nothing was to be lost by signing. The mother of one of the Kerry boys in the hut where I visited Moriarty was ill, and the neighbours had written begging him to come home and see her before she died. His mother was a widow, and there was a large family to be looked after. Finally there came a wire that said: "Mother dying come at once," but he still refused to sign, and his decision was regarded as a proper one. It caught me in my most vulnerable spot. I knew if Mother was dying and that this were my only opportunity of seeing her, I would eat the damn declaration if necessary. I kept on asking everybody I met: "Would you do it?" and found very few prepared to say they wouldn't sign. I appealed to a friend in the camp command to get an order issued that the boy should sign, so as to clear him among his friends, but, like transferring Murphy from one hut to another, this was contrary to principle. I said bitterly that it was a great pity God hadn't made mothers with the durability of principles.

The mother, being of softer material, died, and her younger children, left homeless, were taken in by the neighbours. Now, it was not the possible death of my own mother that I was thinking of so much as that other day when she and her little sister were thrown on to the roadside by bailiffs. I cursed the inhumanity of the two factions with their forms and scruples. At the same time the boy's companions apparently began to realize that his refusal to sign the form and their encouragement was not altogether the grandiose gesture they had thought it, because they concealed from him what had happened. One day as he was wandering down beside his hut and the windows were open, he heard his name mentioned and stopped to listen. He waited until the conversation ended and then, without hesitation, walked straight across the compound towards the barbed wire. A sentry in one of the tall watch-towers had his rifle raised to fire when a military policeman ran up, shouting at him. The policeman put his arm about the boy and brought him back to his hut. When the policeman had gone the boy said: "They wouldn't even shoot me," and began to drop into silence and melancholia; and still, no one had sense enough to make him sign the declaration and go home before it was too late. No wonder I hadn't much patience with my room-mate.

And then the whole business turned sinister. It was announced that all prisoners in the country would take a pledge not to eat until they died or were released. I didn't know whether the morality or the expediency of this scheme was the worse. We professed to be prisoners of war, but the government to which we gave allegiance would accept no responsibility for us, either by surrendering or coming to terms with the enemy. The idea that thousands of men would keep such a pledge to the point at which mass deaths would threaten the existence of the Free State Government seemed to me absurd. Mass martyrdom was only another example of the Shelleyan fantasy, though there were plenty on our side to whom it wasn't even a fantasy but a vulgar political expedient to break the stalemate caused by De Valera's Ceasefire Order.

Walsh, Buckley, and myself let it be understood that we would not take part in the hunger strike. We did not like doing this, because we knew that our position among a thousand men who were hunger-striking for their freedom would be much worse than that of the average blackleg in a plant of the same size. Though we had the blessing of Moriarty and the Limerick men who were joining the strike, we knew it would not be much use to us if things got really dirty. A meeting of the men would have to be held to confirm the decision, and we announced that we should all speak at this, purely to put our purpose on record. This apparently caused some alarm, for at the last moment we were told that the resolution initiating the strike would not be put before a general meeting but before meetings of county groups, so that between us we would only be able to address the Cork, Clare, and Kildare men, leaving ninety per cent of the prisoners unaware that there were objections to the strike. Then

Buckley was served with an order exempting him from the strike because of his youth. I am sure it was done merely with the purpose of protecting him if we were attacked, but he thought otherwise, and replied that he did not propose to avail himself of it and would not join the strike for conscientious reasons. I was impressed by his presence of mind. If it had been I, I should not have seen the consequences of the order until it was too late to clarify my position to anybody.

To make things worse, I was ill with bronchitis, and our own doctor—one of the prisoners—had advised me to go to the hospital. Before I went I attended the Cork meeting and made my speech. I was listened to in silence, and the resolution was passed with only my vote against it. The other two had the same experience. They took me to the main gate on my way to the hospital at the other side of the wire. I was sorry now that I had agreed to go, because I felt I was deserting them.

That night in the hospital a military policeman led in a tall country boy with a vacant expression who had to be undressed and put to bed. Even before the policeman said anything, I knew it was the Kerry boy whose mother had died, and that already his mind had begun to give way. I did not sleep much. I would hear a heavy sigh and a stir of clothes and then the Kerryman would slip quietly out of bed and pad across the floor to a window. He climbed on the sill and stood there in his short shirt, his arms outstretched, his face crushed between the bars. He would remain like that for several minutes, and then give another deep sigh and return to his bed. A couple of times when I woke it was to see him there like that, caught in the blaze of the big searchlight, his arms outstretched, and I could not help thinking of the crucifixion.

I knew nothing about mental illness, but I understood that boy's as though I had been responsible for it myself. I felt that if I had done to my mother what he had innocently done to his, I should be in the same state as he was, so crushed by guilt that I should be unable to think of anything else and searching frantically for any dark corner of my mind where I could take refuge from the dreadful gramophone record that went on repeating itself as though it would never stop. For hours next day I sat by his bed, trying to talk to him. I found that with persistence I could get him to follow a simple conversation in a fairly lucid way, but the moment the conversation veered even for an instant towards his home and family he slumped into vacancy again, and each time it was harder to rouse him. Next day they took him away—to a mental hospital, I was told.

Meanwhile I could get no treatment nor even a discharge. Only a military doctor could discharge me, and he rarely appeared. When he did drop in a couple of days later I was mad with frustration and insisted on going back to the camp. It was a bitter, black day; the compound was a sea of mud and apparently deserted, since most of the hunger-strikers had taken to their beds to keep warm. I had a message from one of the hospital patients for a friend in the Cork hut, and I was shocked at the changes in it. Partitions and doors had been torn down to keep the stoves going, big cans of water were steaming on the stoves, and the men were lying in or on their beds unshaven, with mugs of hot salt water beside them. This was supposed to stay the craving for food. Those who were still up and dressed were shivering over the stoves, dishevelled and gloomy. But it was the silence that struck me most —all that busy hammering, singing, and chatter ended. The men avoided my eyes, and as I went out I was followed by a general hiss. I had apparently got back in time to see things turn really ugly.

There was no change in my friends of the Limerick hut. Nothing seemed able to suppress their high spirits, and when I came back from the dining hall with my tinware under my blue coat to avoid giving offence, they yelled for a full report on the meal and started to plan ideal menus for the evening of their release and ideal girls to share them with. But though I didn't realize it, there was already a change. Next day a small group of Corkmen—some of whom had hissed me the previous day—gave in, and when I reached the dining hall there was an ugly scene as they pleaded for food, and the kitchen staff told them arrogantly that they must give twenty-four hours notice. Walsh, Buckley, and I gave them our food. One of them asked shyly: "Do you remember the day we rescued you in Kilmallock?" It was his way of reminding me that he had not always been so abject a figure and had done his stint of soldiering as well as the rest. He did not have to justify himself to me. I felt like killing somebody.

I was blamed for this collapse, quite without justification, because Walsh, Buckley, and myself had already agreed that once the strike began we should say nothing to influence anybody. I got the *Irish Statesman*, which was sent me by a Quaker friend, and that week it contained one of the most furious articles that its editor, George Russell, ever wrote, denouncing the hunger strike. This, too, we decided to keep to ourselves, though Moriarty always got the paper after me.

That evening an order was issued that I must leave the Limerick hut, live by myself in a room sealed off from one of the bigger huts, and not enter any

268

other. The Limerick men wanted me to ignore it, and offered to deal with any force that was sent to eject me, but I felt they already had enough trouble on their hands. Buckley insisted on moving in with me, and, when I protested, said quietly: "Oh, no, they're trying to break us up." The baby of the group was growing up with great rapidity.

There was nothing in the order to prevent me speaking to my own friends, so that evening at dusk I went to see' Moriarty and talked with him through the window. He and his three room-mates were in bed, drinking salt water. I sat on the window-ledge in the rain, and he began to complain of the delay in bringing him the *Irish Statesman*. I told some lie about having left it behind me in the hospital, but he didn't believe me.

"You didn't bring it because there's an attack on us in it," he said, and I had to admit he was right.

"Is it bad?"

"Pretty bad. Cathal and Tom also thought you'd better not read it."

"Oh, we'll read it," he said in his gentle lazy way. "We're four sick men, but if you don't bring that paper down tonight, we're going up for it."

Just then a file of soldiers passed behind me in the rainy dusk with a military policeman at their head. Two burst in the door of Moriarty's room, took the mugs of salt water from beside the beds, and threw the contents past me into the compound. Then they filled them with hot soup from a bucket. Before they could leave the room, Moriarty, mad with rage, jumped out of bed and emptied the soup after the salt water. I went back to my room, took the *Irish Statesman* and tossed it in the window to him.

Next morning, as Buckley and I were on our way

to the dining hall with our plates under our coats, Moriarty and his three room-mates staggered out to join us with their plates and mugs in their hands. One of them told me that Moriarty had read the article aloud to them without comment and then asked: "Are we as mad as this fellow thinks?" "We are," said one, and the other two agreed. I knew then that the strike was over. The others who had given in were only poor, shamed, and frightened boys to whom nobody paid attention, but Moriarty was a natural leader, and no one who followed his example need regard himself as a weakling. The strike had now become a mere endurance test, and already there was a different tone in the dining hall. The kitchen staff, who fed like restaurant cats, had maintained a tone of chilly disapproval to conscientious objectors and contempt and scorn to defaulters, but now they were on the defensive, waving their arms and shouting that they couldn't produce food without notice. The defaulters had ceased to be mere individuals and become a class.

But the strike dragged on for days before the master minds of the revolution saw that their organization was bleeding to death under their eyes and issued a hasty general dispensation. Immediately the whole camp became hysterical. Even the sentries dropped their rifles and dragged buckets of soup to the barbed wire, and the prisoners tore their hands as they thrust their mugs through it, pushing and shouldering one another out of the way. Some got sick but came back for more. A tall, spectacled man who had not been invited to join the strike came up to me with an oily smile. "Well, professor," he said gleefully, "the pigs feed," and I turned away in disgust because that was exactly what the scene resembled, and I knew it was the end of our magical improvisation. Buckley, Walsh, and myself looked on as though it were the funeral of someone we loved, and when we could bear it no more we went off by ourselves to the other side of the camp. We had reason for complacency, but there was no complacency in us. We knew we should never again find ourselves with so many men we respected and we felt their humiliation as though it were our own. In the years to come, travelling through the country, I would meet with the survivors of the period—some of the best, like Walsh, I should not meet because they took off early for America. "The Lost Legion" I called them. There they were in small cities and towns, shopkeepers or civil servants, bewildered by the immensity of the disaster that had overwhelmed them, the death-in-life of the Nationalist Catholic establishment, and after a few minutes I would hear the cry I had so often heard before—"The country! Oh, God, the bloody country!"

That same day another mass meeting was held. This time there was no nonsense about individual county meetings because one of them, out of sheer cantankerousness, might have voted to continue the strike, and the strike was over. I didn't bother to attend it, but Walsh brought an account of it. Everyone congratulated everyone else on the superhuman endurance and discipline that had been displayed and exonerated those who had abandoned the strike on their own responsibility. But this was anti-climax, and everyone knew it. The camp was a grave of lost illusions; amid the ruin of their huts it was impossible to get the men to take pride in their duties, and the school practically disbanded for lack of students. Nobody thought any longer but of how soon release might come for himself.

We had had a foretaste of what that meant. Two

audacious girls, realizing that fighting was over and that no one was likely to kill them in cold blood, walked coolly across the fields one evening from the main road and stood outside the wire by the Limerick hut, asking for some relative. In their high tower the sentries fumed, waiting for a military policeman to escort the girls away. In no time a crowd gathered, and two or three men who knew the girls stood on the grass bank overlooking the wire and talked to them. The rest of us stood or sat around in complete silence. It was years since some of the group had heard a woman's voice. Nobody cracked a dirty joke; if anyone had, I think he might have been torn asunder. This was sex in its purest form, sex as God may perhaps have intended it to be—a completion of human experience, unearthly in its beauty and staggering in its triviality. "Mother said to ask did you get the cake. Jerry Deignan's sister asked to be remembered to you."

One bright cold November day after I had been in prison for almost a year, I was sitting in Walsh's room when the Limerick hut-leader burst in and said: "Come on, Michael! You're being released." He was a small, brusque, slightly pompous and very kindly man. I didn't move. It was a favourite joke, though not one I should have expected from him, and I felt I must not give myself away. "Come on, I tell you! The officer is waiting," he said impatiently, and Walsh went pale and smiled and said in a low voice, "That's right, Michael. You're wanted." I still could not believe it. Walsh accompanied me to my room, but the officer had gone, and suddenly I did believe it and wanted to cry. "Oh, he'll be back," the hut-leader said testily. "Why don't you get your things together?" My shirt and underpants were drying on a line outside the hut but I could not be bothered to take them. Shaking all over, I made a parcel of my little library—my sixpenny anthologies of German and Spanish poetry, my anthology of Gaelic poetry, my beloved Heine, *Hermann und Dorothea,* and a school history of the Crusades in French— all that had kept me in touch with the great world of culture that I hoped I might some day belong to. Suddenly the door opened and a green-clad figure asked: "Is O'Donovan here?" That was how they came to call you before a firing squad, and I fancy the sensation was very similar. Too big to be apprehended, it left you stunned and weak and wanting to cry.

I was too bewildered to feel anything at parting from Walsh, who carried my parcel to the front gate, and I felt ashamed. After the usual signing of forms in the front office, I was given the travel vouchers for the little group that was being released with me, and as the camp gate opened and let us through on to a narrow country road with high hedges that led to the station, I realized that it was something of a responsibility, for I could feel in myself the same hysteria that swept through my little group. When they heard the sound of a car they looked round and cracked morbid jokes about being re-taken, and I could see them measuring the hedges at either side, wondering if they could run for it. I understood it perfectly because I wanted to get into the fields and then run like mad. Run and run and run and never stop! For the first time I felt the presence of that shadow line that divides the free man from the prisoner.

I had difficulty at the refreshment centre our women had set up in a little cottage by the road. Though I explained that there would be no train for an hour, the men did not want to go in. They wanted to go back on to the main road and bum a lift. Two of them actually did. When the rest had been reassured, we had sandwiches and tea, and the girls who ran the refreshment centre escorted us to the little seaside station. The small local train from Drogheda came in, and, seeing a young woman with a baby in one carriage, I climbed in beside them, and all the way to Dublin I scarcely took my eyes from the baby. Even the lovely open sea in evening light did not distract me. I am bad with men, indifferent with women, but I can no more pass a baby than a bookstore. All that year I had been missing what Pearse was to remember on the eve of his execution, "things bright and green, things young and happy."

The girls had arranged rooms for us in a hotel in Parnell Square because there was no train to Cork. It was late when I reached home next day, and, after the first excitement of home-coming was over, Mother suddenly burst into tears and said: "It made a man of you." It was one of those remarks she often dropped that puzzled and upset me, because the context was always missing, and I had noticed no change at all in myself unless it was the urgent realization of the importance of grammar, particularly the accusative case. Now I know that she saw some change in me and was glad that I was at last a man, though she could not help grieving for the awkward adolescent who had been so helplessly dependent on her. All that really mattered to me was being home again, where I could see her and talk to her about my plans for the future, and sleep in the little pink-washed attic she had made so neat for me, and sit by the orange-box that served me for a bookcase and flick through the pages of books I had been separated from so long that I had forgotten their very existence. It did not even matter to me that while I was in gaol I had won the first prize in the national competition for a critical essay on Turgenev in

Irish—a prize that Corkery had won a couple of years
before—which was just as well, because that year the
national festival went bust, and I never got the seven
pounds that would have meant so much to me. Anyway it pleased Father because it meant that sooner
or later the writing might bring in some money.

But the following Sunday I found I did not want
to go to Mass, and at the first and only political meeting I attended, Corkery had to rescue me from a young
man who called me a traitor. After that, it was friends
who believed I had done wrong in opposing the hunger
strike, and a girl who said bitterly when I met her in
the street: "I hear you don't believe in God any longer." Though this wasn't true, it took me some time to
realize what Mother had seen in that first glimpse of
me, that I had crossed another shadow line, and make
me wonder if I should ever again be completely at ease
with the people I loved, their introverted religion and
introverted patriotism. I suspect she saw it all, in the
way that mothers do, and understood the consequences for me better than I have ever been able to
do. Thirty years later, when she was not far from her
death, I spoke to her about the possibility of my having
to leave Ireland and—knowing her hatred of leaving
home—suggested that I might get a place for her in
Cork. "Of course I'll go with you," she said without a
moment's hesitation. "I know you must be free. Life
without freedom is nothing." To her, of course, "freedom" did not mean freedom to do what one pleased—
that was a conception that never crossed her mind—
but freedom to do what one thought "right," whatever
the consequences. She left me bewildered then, as she
had so often left me bewildered before. It was strange
to hear an old woman of eighty-five, an orphan, a
servant girl who had never had anything she could

really call her own, speak with the very voice of Antigone.

All our arguments about the immortality of the soul seem to me to be based on one vast fallacy—that it is our vanity that desires eternity. Vanity! As though any reasonable man could be vain enough to believe himself worth immortality! From the time I was a boy and could think at all, I was certain that for my own soul there was only nothingness. I knew it too well in all its commonness and weakness. But I knew that there were souls that were immortal, that even God, if He wished to, could not diminish or destroy, and perhaps it was the thought of these that turned me finally from poetry to story-telling, to the celebration of those who for me represented all I should ever know of God. My mother was merely one among them, though, in my human weakness, I valued her most, and now that I am old myself, I remember the line of a psalm (probably mistranslated) that has always been with me since I read it first:

"And when I wake I shall be satisfied with Thy likeness."

New York, 1958–1960

A NOTE ON THE AUTHOR

AFTER THIS BOOK nothing need be added about the first twenty years in the life of Frank O'Connor (Michael O'Donovan). Following his release from prison, he met AE, who published poems, stories, and translations by him in the *Irish Statesman*. His first published book was *Guest of the Nation*, a volume of short stories. He has published novels, several additional volumes of tales, *The Mirror in the Roadway* (a study of the modern novel), verse, travel books, and a study of Michael Collins and the Irish Revolution. In recent years he has lived mostly in the United States, and has taught at Harvard, Northwestern, and Stanford universities. The first volume of his collected (and largely rewritten) stories—*The Stories of Frank O'Connor*—was published in 1952, the second—*More Stories by Frank O'Connor*—in 1954. Further stories, *Domestic Relations*, appeared in 1957, and in 1959 he published *Kings, Lords, and Commons*, an anthology of Irish poetry from 600 A.D. to the nineteenth century which he translated.

January 1961

A NOTE ON THE TYPE

THE TEXT of this book was set on the Linotype in a new face called PRIMER, designed by *Rudolph Ruzicka,* earlier responsible for the design of Fairfield and Fairfield Medium. The design of the face makes general reference to Linotype Century, but brilliantly corrects the characterless quality of that face.